Turning Points

Turning Points

How to Handle
Change in Your Life

Mary Carroll Moore

ECKANKAR
Minneapolis, MN

Turning Points: How to Handle Change in Your Life

Copyright © 1995 Mary Carroll Moore

The terms ECKANKAR, ECK, EK, MAHANTA, SOUL TRAVEL, and VAIRAGI, among others, are trademarks of ECKANKAR, P.O. Box 27300, Minneapolis, MN 55427 U.S.A.

Printed in U.S.A.

Edited by Joan Klemp and Anthony Moore

Back cover photo by The Studio Central

Library of Congress Cataloging-in-Publication Data

Moore, Mary Carroll.
    Turning points : how to handle change in your life / Mary Carroll Moore.
        p. cm.
    Includes bibliographical references.
    ISBN 1-57043-102-7 (perfect bound : alk. paper)
    1. Eckankar (Organization)—Doctrines. 2. Spiritual life.
I. Title
BP605.E3M65 1995
299'.93—dc20   95-6396
                                            CIP

Contents

Acknowledgments

Special thanks to Beverly and Zanna, my weekly writing group; my husband, Tony, for suggesting the title of the book and giving me many months of encouragement as I wrote and rewrote; and all the friends who shared their personal stories.

I have changed the names of private individuals in my stories to protect their privacy. If any of these names belong to any person, living or dead, it is pure coincidence.

Introduction

When I was nineteen I took a trip across the U.S. by myself. I drove a little VW bug I'd named Bessie.

It was my first car, bought after working all summer in a natural foods restaurant in Baltimore. The excitement of the trip was not knowing ahead of time which route I would take. I only knew I wanted to get to Texas to meet a friend the following week.

One afternoon I was driving through the rolling terrain of the Ozark foothills when the road emptied onto a shallow lake. This was a surprise. Across the lake I could see the pinpoint of highway continue. But how was I to get across?

I waited on the shore for about fifteen minutes. When cars behind me started lining up, I realized there was probably a ferry that operated on the lake and carried cars to the far side.

The ferry did arrive. We drove on board carefully, lining up our vehicles on the railless platform. Part of me was afraid to drive my little car onto that ferry. What if a wind came up, and the lake turned choppy.

I imagined one dip of the boat and the whole line of cars sliding off the edge.

But I needed to cross, and there was no other road. So I found a spot toward the middle, in back of a Cadillac from Missouri. As the ferry's engines began to grind, the boat slid back into the wide expanse of water.

I stayed in the car, still gripping the steering wheel, even though it was hot and the scant breeze through the open window barely touched the car's steamy interior. But noticing how the ferry moved so evenly across the lake's surface reassured me.

Finally I opened the car door and stepped out to stretch, breathe deeply of the pine-scented air, and chat with other drivers who were also emerging from their cars.

As the ferry moved around one of the lake's small islands, a panorama opened up before us. It was close to sunset, and the hills were turning purple; the sky was a deepening blue, almost indigo, with pine trees silhouetted against it.

I felt a surging sensation in my chest, a feeling of being touched by pure beauty, almost more than I could bear.

I knew that moment was a turning point in my life.

The metaphors were obvious: coming to a significant crossroads at sunset—the ending of one cycle and the beginning of another. A road ending. Crossing unfamiliar territory to take up another. Fears surfacing as I cling to the familiar for a while until I am reassured that my passage was safe. Then I step out to breathe deeply.

There are many such roads in life. You may be driving down one when it empties onto a lake or simply changes directions suddenly. Signs may appear to warn you of a detour ahead, that you must make a change.

Most experienced drivers easily navigate a highway detour, but many of us have difficulty navigating personal changes, our turning points. We may close our eyes in fear of the change. We may make the turn too late. We may say, "I don't want to get off the road I've been traveling!" and grip the steering wheel even tighter.

But there is a way to become a coworker with change.

Working from the highest viewpoint, the Soul viewpoint, we can view change as beneficial and learn to flow with it rather than struggle against it. To have success with change means practicing basic spiritual skills: trust, faith, inner listening, awareness. Even major life shifts—birth, death, marriage, divorce—can be navigated more easily with these skills.

I've found that there is one constant in life: change. We cannot escape change. It is inevitable.

We travel through life learning, growing, and changing. Without change we would die. Resisting change is about as futile as refusing to get on the ferry that will carry you across the lake.

"A turning point is life's way of giving you a chance to move ahead spiritually," writes Sri Harold Klemp, the spiritual leader of ECKANKAR. This book will show how to look for and use the spiritual turning points in your life, and how they can help you live with more creativity, with less fear, with more joy.

You might even begin to enjoy the challenge of new experience, to welcome the unexpected growth and joy.

The first step is learning how to recognize your own turning points—as well as major life themes—and use them to welcome change instead of trying to avoid it.

1. What Are Turning Points?

With the economy at a low point several years ago, there was no way I wanted to leave my comfortable job. But lately I had been experiencing a vague restlessness, anxiety, and health problems at work. It was the first job I had held for longer than a few years. I loved my work, editing and compiling books for several authors, but suddenly I was feeling unhappy about Monday mornings and couldn't wait for weekends. Not only that but I began to develop strange numbness and pain in my right arm which severely limited my time on the computer. My productivity was falling fast.

Having worked with turning points for many years helped me recognize the signs that a change was needed.

In the past, my first guess would be: Time to move on. But my husband and I had just bought a bigger house with a bigger mortgage, and my freelance writing business, while healthy, was not bringing in enough to replace my salary. Besides, my work was valued and leaving could put the office in a very tight spot.

At first I couldn't imagine what else life could be trying to tell me. Wasn't I receiving my usual sign that it was time to move on? Why else would I be feeling the familiar restlessness?

And my job could be the only possible candidate for change. My marriage, my writing career, and other areas of my life were in great shape. They caused me no concern at the moment.

One night after a very frustrating day at work, with such discomfort in my right arm that computer time was limited to fifteen-minute stretches, I asked my husband if he thought I should leave my job. He looked at me for a long moment then said, "It does seem you're ready to change something. But what if life is telling you to change yourself rather than your job?"

My approach to turning points had always been: (1) read the signs of anxiety and restlessness that point to coming change and (2) look around for something outside myself to alter.

Was it possible this turning point was different?

A conversation with another woman on the editing team flashed across my mind. Earlier that day we had been talking about a book I was working on; I had told her about my arm and how it was delaying delivery of the chapters. "What a relief," she had laughed, to my surprise. "I was having trouble keeping up with you!"

Always a speedy worker, I had a tendency to plan way ahead and fairly rush through my days. I was often exhausted by this pace, but I had always prided myself on my output level. Between my arm slowing me down and my coworker's hint that she *wanted* me to slow down, it looked as if my pace was needing to be adjusted. Perhaps my pattern of rushing had been a benefit for a long time but had become an obstacle: something that was making me spiritually sick and perhaps physically too.

I decided to keep an eye out for more signs of the coming turning point. One came the very next day.

I had arranged to spend my lunch hour shopping with two friends from the office. The drive took about twenty minutes, so we talked about work on the way. One woman chatted about how she was so glad to have me as a role model. "What for?" I asked.

"Learning how to slow down," she said.

I had told her nothing about my conversation with my husband the night before. In my stunned silence, she added that she used to feel like a machine at work, always busy producing. Now she saw how she was able to serve in her job in other ways, by just being there for people and taking the time to relax and pace herself better.

"You know, I've always valued that quality in you," she said, turning around in her seat to look at me. Me? In my present state I felt far removed from the serenity she was talking about.

But her words struck me deeply. Through my study of ECKANKAR, I'd become keenly aware of the ways Divine Spirit often speaks to us through ordinary conversations.

An even more direct sign came the next morning. I had set up an appointment with an acupuncturist about my arm, since the other avenues of medical doctors and chiropractors had not helped the pain and numbness. The first thing the acupuncturist asked when he looked at me was: "Have you been pushing too hard?"

OK, I thought, *enough is enough. I get the message.* Life was trying so hard to tell me what I needed to change. With very blatant signals, it was telling me I didn't need to quit my job, I needed to change my whole approach to my work.

That night before I went to sleep, I wrote a message to Divine Spirit in my dream journal: "I know I need to change my pace. I know I am hurting myself by the speed at which I'm living. But I don't know how to navigate this turning point. Please help me tonight in my dreams."

The next morning I woke up with only a vague memory of my dream state. But three phrases kept drifting across my attention that day, and I knew they were the keys to making this important change.

In the months that followed, I practiced these three keys. The first was to do everything with careful attention to detail. As soon as I began to pay attention to the small details and not to finishing each task as fast as I could, I realized I was slowing down. It was a natural thing.

The second was: enjoy the process, rather than the result. I realized I had been so result-focused, I had lost my enjoyment of my work. No wonder I was bored and unhappy.

The third was the most simple: when I found myself feeling pushed or tense inside, I was to breathe very deeply.

Walk the Walk

When I decided to write this book, my purpose was to show others how to approach turning points

4

with a new attitude. Right away, life had given me a chance to walk the walk: to practice what I was writing about.

Determining the direction of this turning point with my job showed me how closely life works with us during change. Like crossing a strange lake on a ferry, we are often confronted with something we need to traverse in order to grow. A turning point is a window of spiritual opportunity. And each turning point is always preceded by signs that alert us to the coming change and ask us gently to make an adjustment.

There's usually a gap between the arrival of a turning point and the fulfillment stage where we begin settling in to the new state of consciousness.

In *Ask the Master,* Book Two, Sri Harold Klemp writes, "Each life cycle has a growth and fulfillment stage. We switch back and forth between them. The growth phase begins with a restless feeling that urges us into a new and greater opportunity, but fear holds us back. Finally, this need for growth outweighs the fear."

At that point we begin to consider accepting the spiritual opportunity of the turning point.

We begin looking at how to take the necessary steps and face the risks we must take in order to grow. Fulfillment comes as we allow the new skills to become part of ourselves, as we "master the new routines and plunge into the options of our unexplored life," as Sri Harold says.

Life is a series of these cycles, from childhood into old age. It's a natural process. But certain people are able to flow with the cycles of growth and change, make decisions and choose what to do, realizing that change is a part of life that must be embraced.

Rather than being victimized by change, they see the options of life and are intrigued by the opportunities of turning points.

Fear is often a constant companion, even for those skilled in recognizing turning points. But courage can be constant too.

"Courage is resistance to fear, mastery of fear—not absence of fear," Mark Twain once said. Courage walks hand in hand with stepping into new areas of living. It comes when we begin to use our creative resources to face and make the change.

Strong Vision

Change is frightening because it takes us into the unfamiliar.

Unless we have a strong vision of what lies ahead and are convinced that we are able to survive no matter what happens to us, we tremble at the thought of reaching outside our comfort zone. We tremble at taking the risk of venturing into the unknown.

A friend of mine dreamed of working full-time in the world of food, but had a secure position as a computer programmer. As she assisted me in my cooking classes, she'd often talk about how much she loved creating and testing recipes, trying new foods, and working with people in the food world. But jobs that would give her all that were scarce.

To make the change to the job of her dreams, she would have to be very creative. She would also have to face self-doubt and fear.

There was always the possibility of failure, something that rarely happened in the secure environment of her present life. But she realized her present security was also beginning to feel like a prison, and she decided to challenge her creativity. So she started looking for work in the new field.

In a few months, she was asked to assist a cookbook author, testing recipes in a beautiful and well-equipped kitchen. She quit her computer job and was soon working full-time in the world of food.

When I asked my friend how she had managed to make the leap, she said that despite her fears, she had held on to her dream of what she wanted. Her inner vision had been strong. Her ability to dream a dream of what she really wanted—and hold a strong, yet flexible vision—brought her through the turning point and changed her life.

☀ Exercise: Dream Your Dream

To develop a strong vision, try this exercise. Take a minute and imagine your next step: a dream job, friendship, love relationship, or house—whatever you feel would bring you more of what you want in life.

Close your eyes and get a good feeling, image, or sense of it. Take five minutes, and write or draw everything you can about this image. Especially important: include the *qualities* the image brings, how it makes you feel.

Now put the paper away for six months. In six months look at what you wrote; you may be surprised at what has happened with your dream.

Each time I have tried this exercise, I have been amazed at what this kind of dreaming can achieve.

Cocreator or Victim?

In order to bring the benefit of turning points into our lives, we have to be able to see ourselves as cocreators rather than victims. Like my friend in the earlier story, we have to be able to dream a dream and believe it can be fulfilled.

Maybe there are a host of fears standing in the way, like a wide lake without a ferry to cross it. We have to be able to believe that the ferry is just around the bend, chugging its way toward us.

The first step is to begin dreaming, but the attitude we hold about our chances for success also plays a big part.

Many people feel victimized and cannot dream a new future beyond their present one because they are immobilized by a dragging-the-feet kind of fear. They cannot seem to take the action needed to move toward what they want. They have adopted an attitude of helplessness, the victim of life's battering. Change always surprises and distresses the victim.

Being a victim means that you lay facedown and let life run right over you. Not only does it hurt, playing the victim keeps you from looking around and seeing the turning points that may offer new opportunities.

In the victim role, there is often an unconscious (or very out-in-the-open) wish to move on. But the fear is too strong—you want life or someone else to make the decision for you. Two close friends experienced this recently with jobs they hated but were afraid to leave. They both knew management was tightening its belt, and unless they showed more enthusiasm for their jobs, they would be laid off. Not long after, they were.

There's another kind of fear of change that is equally common. It manifests as changing simply for the sake of change. These people have no trouble dreaming the dream. They can dream many dreams. But change is so intoxicating that they rarely will stick with a dream long enough to see it manifest.

Changing for the sake of change is a paradox: it actually avoids any real or lasting growth. By making erratic changes you never settle into a commitment to work things out. There is lots of movement but also the feeling that you are getting nowhere. You may be cheating yourself out of the growth and experience that comes with commitment.

Ralph Keyes, in *Chancing It,* describes two types of risk-takers. Level I risk-takers like outwardly challenging activities like starting their own businesses, performing in public, taking up skydiving or other thrill sports. Someone comfortable with outwardly challenging activities may be the change-for-change's-sake type of person, quite nervous when it comes to making true inner change. Turning points for these people would likely involve settling down and creating something lasting.

Level II risk-takers are rarely as inclined toward the dramatic. They take risks that present, as Keyes says, "more danger to the spirit than to the body," such as getting married, starting a family, or slowly building a long-term career.

For either type of person, true, beneficial change is usually a lengthy process rather than one sudden movement. It works in harmony with life, with other people for the most part, with your truest goals for yourself.

It takes you somewhere. Often it involves a spiritual element, such as a higher realization about yourself.

☀ Exercise: The Fear Room

Since fear is often part of any reaction to change— whether we tend toward the victim or the change-for-change's-sake attitude—it is helpful to clean out the fear before embarking in a new direction. This exercise has helped me many times.

Close your eyes and breathe deeply for a few moments to relax any tension inside.

Imagine you're looking through a window into a small room. It's dark inside and filled with fog, a fog so dense that it's hard for you to make out the shapes of any objects.

Behind you is a large truck. A machine is being unloaded by some burly men. They wheel the machine up to a hole in the outside wall of the room and attach a long tube, like a vacuum-cleaner hose. One of them flicks a switch, and you watch as all the fog is slowly sucked out of the room.

Then the men unhook the machine, load it back onto the truck, and drive off.

Walk into the room and look around. The fog is completely gone. There's a pleasant fragrance in the air and a light, pleasing sound you can barely hear.

Go to each of the five large windows in the room, and open the shades, allowing sunshine to flood in.

The room symbolizes the inner bodies that are filled with fear. Sometimes when I am facing a

10

turning point that frightens me, I do this exercise several times a week. Each time I try it, the inner room is filled with the fog of fear. But I find that when I clean out the inner fog, my heart feels lighter. Getting rid of fear is often the first step.

In the next chapter, we'll explore step two: how working from the highest viewpoint is essential when you begin working with the turning points in your life.

2. Working with Change from Soul's Viewpoint

Most of us, when turning points hit unexpectedly, cry out, "Why me?" Or "Why now, just when things are getting so good?"

Focused only on what's happening in our smaller world, we wonder at God's imperfect timing. If we were able to look from a higher viewpoint—one that stretched far forward and backward in time—we could see the threads connecting this turning point with the next. Having gained an overview, we would be able to see the ferry coming around the bend.

As Soul, we can each have this overview.

Many modern and ancient writings speak of Soul, the eternal being that never dies. And that with reincarnation, Soul simply chooses a life to learn certain lessons and then moves on to the next life, the next lesson.

Soul also has the ability to move serenely from one experience to the next, without fear and judgment.

My most successful times of weathering turning points have been when I was able to maintain this higher consciousness, this viewpoint of Soul—when I was able to believe that all is for my own good, that there is an order and beauty to the universe. I can operate consciously within that order and beauty if I pay attention, keeping this higher viewpoint. The ECK, Divine Spirit, has each of our lives in Its care.

With the eyes and ears of Soul we are able to receive guidance from this spiritual force, and we can see and hear Its directions most clearly. Many people are confused, however, between the concepts of being Soul versus having a soul. These people talk about my soul, my higher self. But you *are* Soul, you *are* the Higher Self.

Who am I really? I am Soul. As Soul, I have a body, mind, and emotions. Let's try a simple exercise to explore this further.

☀ Exercise: Perceiving Yourself as Soul

Close your eyes and imagine yourself standing in a hallway by a green door.

Beside the door is a coatrack. You notice you are wearing a heavy overcoat. Since it is hot and the coat weighs on your shoulders, you decide to take it off. You do so and hang the coat on the coatrack.

Immediately the door before you swings open. You walk through.

The scene is replayed four more times. Each time you find yourself in front of a door and a coatrack. Each time you are wearing a coat.

The first door was green, and the coat was heavy. It symbolized the Physical Plane and the dense physical body. The second door is pink; your coat is slightly lighter. This symbolizes the Astral Plane and the Emotional body. The third door is orange,

14

the coat lighter still, symbolizing the Causal Plane and the body of past-life recall, memories, and seed ideas. The fourth door is a deep blue; the coat is thick but not heavy. It symbolizes the Mental body and your thoughts.

When you have removed the last coat and walked through the last door, you find yourself in a brightly lit room. The light is pale golden yellow. You have no coat on your shoulders to weigh you down. You feel light and free.

This is you, Soul. Soul wears the physical body, the emotions, the memory, and the mind like the coats we wear in winter for protection. Soul needs protection in the harsh worlds of the lower planes.

The key is to be able to work from this light, high consciousness as you truly are, even while wearing these overcoats.

To not be buffeted by change, we must learn to use the higher viewpoint of Soul. A first step is toning an inner muscle: the imagination.

Our Imagination

Soul's greatest faculty is the imagination. An essential step toward learning how to work with personal turning points is learning how to use the imagination. In the following story, I was unknowingly doing just that, as I pursued what looked like a long shot in my writing career.

In 1989 I had been a published magazine writer for twelve years but felt completely stuck.

Inside was a restlessness to move onward, to become a better writer. I wanted to sell my work to bigger, better paying markets with good exposure, but I had no clue as to what I needed to change.

One day in late spring I wrote a goal in my dream journal. I imagined myself writing for publications all over the U.S. and Canada. I saw my writing as clear and interesting, uplifting to the reader's everyday life. This would fulfill my purpose for being a writer.

But what did I need to do to get there? Take a class? Join a writing group?

Stumped, I decided to begin seeing my writing from the higher viewpoint of Soul.

What did this actually mean? I decided to imagine opening my inner eyes to the small clues that might come my way. I also asked God for any opportunity that I might be ready for, since I really didn't know which direction to pursue. Unbeknownst to me, my goal set in motion a series of events that involved many people.

The first was about to enter my life in the form of a phone call from an old friend, Carol, who called about three weeks later.

Carol had authored a very popular natural-foods cookbook, one of the first of the industry. Riding the popularity of this homey style of cooking, she began writing a weekly column on food and health and selling it to newspapers around the country. Thirty papers had picked it up; the column was successful enough to support her for eleven years.

She called me one day in the early summer and casually asked if I would be interested in taking over her column. She was about to retire from weekly deadlines.

Fear and excitement fought for equal time as I struggled to absorb this. I knew absolutely nothing about writing newspaper columns. I had only written features for a relatively small magazine, a very different ball game. But before I discarded the offer, I wanted to check it out inside.

Was this the turning point I had been waiting for in my writing career?

Testing the Turn

As an experiment, I tried closing my eyes and seeing the situation from the highest level I could imagine.

I gently let the concept of taking on the column float around me. As it settled on my shoulders, I felt peaceful, happy, yet on the cutting edge of my present abilities. I knew this turning point would lead my writing into totally new areas. I knew, at that moment, that my future writing career would be greatly affected by the decision I made. It would stretch every skill I had.

As I did this little exercise, I felt a stillness in the air that was familiar. I had encountered it before at the crossroads of major decisions.

But there was also fear lurking in the shadows. If I gave in to the fear, I would probably never grow to be the writer I wanted to become. If I could move beyond any discomfort and fear, I just might. And from this higher viewpoint of Soul, the fear looked smaller, more manageable.

So I finally said yes, putting all the certainty I felt from that high vision into my voice. "When do I start?" I asked her.

"Probably September," she said. "I'll write the editors and introduce you, then you'll have to call them and pitch the idea yourself." Ugh! I thought. I'd always hated selling myself on the phone. But that feeling of certainty was still there. I reasoned I had until September—almost four months—to learn the newspaper-writing game. I would take it a step at a time.

I must admit at this point the money also lured me. Carol had made bundles of money from this once-a-week, one-thousand-word effort. Maybe writing a column would be my ticket to fame and fortune.

A month later, I was having trouble keeping my high vision.

The effort of pulling together the first column had worn me out. I had read every book detailing the art of writing newspaper columns that I could lay my hands on. I had pumped friends for information. I had studied the food sections of major newspapers.

Comparing my writing to the published columnists, I didn't have much hope for a warm reception when I began calling the editors on Carol's list. But the first editor said yes, and I silently whooped with joy. Until her next words: "We'd like to see four sample columns by the end of the month." Four! I had spent a month writing just one!

The next few weeks I worked harder at my writing than I ever had before, cajoling editor friends to give me feedback, rewriting draft after draft of the four sample columns. Finally I had them ready— and the editor liked them! But that was only one editor. From Carol's thirty newspapers, I landed only four contracts in all.

I began to wonder if my viewpoint when making the decision had been that high after all. What if it was a big mistake?

Learning Curves

Learning on the job is never easy, and that first year the learning curve was extremely steep. That year was also the beginning of one of the worst newspaper slumps my editors had ever seen.

Two of the four newspapers hung on and continued to buy my column, earning me a few hundred dollars a month. But when I counted up the hours I spent putting each column together, developing and testing the recipes, and sending it to the two papers, I often wondered why I continued. Was I really improving my writing enough to make this mountain of work worthwhile?

I was too busy to know the answer—to see my writing objectively. Each time I did my short exercise and looked at the situation from Soul's viewpoint, I got reassurance. But down here things looked dicey.

Then one day an editor from a magazine I'd written for since the seventies called me.

She had noticed that the style and quality of my articles had changed in the past year. What had I done differently—taken a crash course? My writing was tighter, cleaner. I said more in fewer words. I made fewer spelling and grammatical errors. In short, she said, I had become one of their best writers. Would I be willing to take on a monthly column?

This was my first sign that Soul's vision was correct—the newspaper column was beginning to pay off. My crash-and-burn apprenticeship in the field of journalism had taught me more than I knew. I had grown enough to warrant the trust of this editor. With tears in my eyes, I gratefully accepted the assignment for the monthly column.

A Major Leap—At Last

The story isn't over yet, but I want to take a break here to recap.

I was beginning to see how to work with turning points from the higher viewpoint of Soul. Soul has no past, no future. Soul lives eternally in the present moment. As Soul I knew that this was the right step. That's why the fear of trying something new—like the column—rarely causes Soul to flinch.

Soul lives only to grow and expand into greater awareness. So challenges are natural.

Turning points are to be embraced, not feared.

From this higher viewpoint, I had seen success in my writing career if I took on the newspaper column. I had imagined this would be instant success, my name in fifty newspapers across the country. But the ECK, Divine Spirit, had something else in mind. It had known that first I needed a crash course in journalism. And It arranged for me to get this training on the job.

The first concrete sign that I was succeeding came with the offer of the magazine column.

By the sixth year—with over three hundred published columns under my belt—writing the newspaper column had become a graceful routine in my week. Topics came easily, I had gotten much better at crafting anecdotes, and my proofreading and editing skills were sharp.

Financially, however, the column was only just pulling its weight. I often discussed with my husband the idea of dropping it and just concentrating on magazine writing. After all, I reasoned, I had learned the lesson of my crash course in journalism.

It was just after such a conversation that the phone rang one afternoon. It was the food editor of a large West Coast newspaper syndicate that I had written to four years earlier. Digging through stacks of old query letters he had come across mine. A columnist on their staff had just canceled, and he thought my topic of healthy eating would be perfect to start the following month!

Could I provide them with a bimonthly column?

I carefully asked how many papers the syndicate serviced. "Eighty-five and growing each week," the editor told me proudly.

As I look back on the six years of apprenticeship, I am so grateful for the higher viewpoint I had when I needed reassurance. Soul said, "Hang in there," even when the mind argued.

And the ECK sent me tiny turning points of encouragement to keep producing the column even when only two papers wanted it. A grateful letter would come from a reader, a friend would call to ask me to teach a writing class on column-writing, my editors would send me encouraging notes or give me an unexpected raise. I'd read an old column and marvel how my writing had improved in the past year.

Sometimes bringing our goals to fruition takes as long as this, or longer. We have to keep our dream strong, our imagination bright. We have to be able to see that the road ahead is going somewhere!

How do we do this?

In the following chapters, we'll explore the key tools that help you hold on to—and work from—this higher viewpoint.

3. Faith in Yourself and Life's Process

A friend had a dream where she was moving into a new home provided by ECKANKAR. The Mahanta, the inner guide, had arranged for some of her old furniture to be moved, plus he had sent over new furniture. When my friend and her husband arrived at the new house, she was amazed but concerned.

"I'll have to work for ECKANKAR the rest of my life to pay for all of this," she said to her husband.

"But look," he said, "it's coming from the sky." Sure enough, the new furniture was falling out of the sky and landing softly inside the home. "Let's see the shipping slips," she argued. "Maybe there is something we don't need."

"Accept it all," her husband said softly. "What we don't need now, we'll store."

My friend was profoundly moved by this dream. It seemed to be saying to her, through the voice of her husband: *Accept the gifts life brings to you.*

A benevolent force was telling her that she was completely taken care of if she would surrender and relax.

In the past, my friend had at times wondered if life was truly on her side. The dream brought her added reassurance that life was here to help her, not hinder her. "It's not that we won't have hardships," she added after telling me the dream. "But hardships don't have to be the point of life."

Such understanding grows as you develop faith in yourself and in God.

Turning Points as Creative Challenge

People who work easily with their turning points usually view these changes as creative challenges, rather than unwelcome stress or disasters. They ask themselves first: How can I make the best of this? How can I discover something new? What is the gift within this experience?

Many of these people have a basic belief: God is looking out for them.

They don't shirk responsibility, but they do believe wholeheartedly that life brings blessings rather than curses. They have a steady faith in life's process — that it continually evolves for good rather than bad.

To this kind of person, change can bring the excitement of discovery rather than dismay. If there's a gift within the experience, a creative person finds it.

"Creative people are often more able to live with tension, including constant change. The excitement of discovery outweighs anxiety over turning one's world upside-down," commented Dr. Wayne Myers of Cornell University Medical Center in a 1989 article in *SELF* magazine.

How do they do this?

Fear is born in the mind, and people who view change as a creative challenge reduce the fear by distracting the mind. They give it a puzzle to solve — a puzzle such as how to make the change work. Intent on solving the puzzle, the mind has little chance to become frozen and immobilized.

One man I spoke with had a useful technique that eased the mind's fear and helped him see his turning points creatively.

He regularly charted his personal growth in his journal. Over the years he had noted how his life worked in a predictable pattern. His growth opportunities came at certain intervals, usually just when he was outgrowing some present circumstance—an inner belief or attitude, a relationship, living quarters, a job.

When a turning point hit, instead of panicking he took time to read through his journal entries for the past two to four months and highlight with a yellow marker anything that seemed to foreshadow the change.

He'd look for restlessness or upsetting experiences, anything unusual in waking experiences or sleeping dreams—signs that might have been nudging him to look more closely at his life. Using this information he was able to prove to himself that advance warning always came before a turning point and gave clues as to the direction to take and choices to make.

Once he was paying attention, valuable insights began to come in dreams, daily experiences, and his contemplation period.

Those who aren't journal keepers can talk about an upcoming change with a friend or family member who knows them well. Have they noticed anything in the months leading up to this turning point? Any pattern found may encourage a person to begin keeping notes to help predict and flow more easily with the next turning point.

It also helps one pay more attention to living in the moment—the place where life signals coming changes.

Living in the Moment

Deepak Chopra, M.D., world-recognized authority on holistic health, says that stress is not so much about present problems: "Instead we feel anxiety because we anticipate pain in the future, or we feel depression, guilt or sorrow because we brood on pain from the past. Freeing yourself of past and future relieves you of stress. . . . It also makes you better able to get things done."

The concept of living in the moment is basic to Soul's survival. I had learned this long ago in the ECKANKAR teachings. But it didn't really hit home until my friend Suzanne told me this story.

She had fallen in love with Bill, who lived in another city.

Bill was planning to move to be with Suzanne, but there were several loose ends to tie up with his business. Not sure if the crucial settlement would go through, Suzanne worried on the phone with Bill about their future. Would they ever be together? Would she have to quit her job and move to be with him? Around and around the conversation went.

Bill finally was silent for a moment, then he said, "Remember, things are OK right now. We're happy now."

Suzanne was struck by the simplicity of this statement. In essence, if they could keep their focus on the present moment, their lives were happy.

Living in the moment means that you do the best you can to take care of future circumstances then place the greater part of your attention right here and now. Once you have done everything you can, you do not worry about losing your job, your spouse, your home.

Once you have prepared as best you can, you do not let your mind stew about what you will do tomorrow.

Joe Bailey, author of *The Serenity Principle,* said, "We are never really *in* the future; we only *think* we are. In fact, we are always in the present, whether our thoughts are of the future or the past."

Living in the moment also means letting go of the past.

In his book *Breathing Space,* Jeff Davidson asks: "What are you waiting for before you're willing to fully engage in life, in this day?" Most people have a list of things where others have "done them wrong." They carry the list around like a heavy overcoat, and it weighs a lot. Worse, it keeps them from paying any attention to turning points in the present.

Unable to focus on the present, they often make the same mistakes over and over again.

Those who can live in the present have done all they can do about the past and are content to let it be in the past. They resolve the things they can, let go of the things they can't. They do everything they agree to do and trust that that is good enough.

If you ignore the present moment, you are missing

out on most of the joy in life. You are also doomed to miss most of the turning points that will show you what to do next.

I practice living in the moment by monitoring worries and negative thoughts, since they are the troublemakers that steal my attention. Whenever a negative thought comes up, I find it helpful to write it down—even if it seems unwise to put attention on it—along with possible resolutions. When it is out of my mind and on paper, it can dissipate more quickly, as in the following exercise.

☀ Exercise: On Dissipating Worry

This is adapted from an exercise called "Write It Down!" in *The Spiritual Exercises of ECK* by Sri Harold Klemp.

To dissipate worry and regain focus in the moment, write a letter (that you never send) to someone you trust. Describe your worry, problem, or negative thought in the first few sentences.

Then keep writing anything that comes to mind. Often you will get at least one small action that you can take to resolve the issue.

As you take this action, you find that it frees you up to focus more attention on the present moment again.

Life Themes

An ECKist in a workshop on keeping a spiritual journal that I led wrote me about a breakthrough from an exercise we did.

In it she had listed twelve major turning points in her life, then wrote for ten minutes about one of them, without censoring or editing herself. When she had written one page, she put the writing away overnight.

She reread it in the morning and discovered an important insight about herself. Throughout the turning point she had written about, the ECK had been gently leading her in a search for spiritual freedom. With a great deal of excitement, she read over the other turning points on her list and saw that nine out of twelve also had themes of spiritual freedom.

A primary life theme was emerging. And she could now see it reflected in each major change she'd experienced since she was a child.

The woman attended an ECK Worship Service that Sunday and was surprised to find the discussion topic was childhood experiences the group most valued. Several people talked about spiritual freedom, and some of them carried it a step further to talk about the responsibility that comes with freedom.

The ECKist was excited to see a common thread running through her life experiences, binding them together.

A master plan was certainly in effect. Seeing this larger plan helped her be aware of the guidance of Divine Spirit. She now knew a primary theme of her life from a spiritual perspective: to find spiritual freedom and learn how to be responsible with it.

Grace under Fire

A life theme of my own emerged when I was using the same exercise.

I realized that most of my turning points in the

past five years had been about learning to move through life with more grace.

Robert Redford wrote about grace as a theme for his 1993 movie on fly-fishing, *A River Runs Through It,* in an article for *Vogue:* "Grace was . . . a tool by which you carved your way to salvation. . . . As Norman McLean says, 'Trout as well as eternal salvation comes by grace, and grace comes by art, and art does not come easy.' "

Grace for me became a way to realize more about God and God's plan for my life. And it did not come easily. The first time I began to be aware of grace as a theme in my life had to do with the first flower garden I planted.

Nature herself takes on most gardeners to teach them a hard lesson in humility. Just when you think you have a handle on the seasons, the weather, and what you can expect to grow where, you are reminded how little control a gardener may have. Experience and skill are not worth much in the face of a freeze in April or a hailstorm in July.

My gardening experiences started soon after I moved to a northern state and bought my first house.

It was a time of uncertainty in my life as well as a time of hope and new beginnings. Here I was, in a land of four definite seasons. A dream came true when I found a home for sale that was small enough and priced right.

The only drawback was the yard.

The house had been unsold for months because of that yard. Although the interior sported new wallpaper, flooring, and carpets—even a few new windows—the outside was scraggly, with patches of decaying plant life, bare soil, and occasional tufts of grass. The previous owners had kept several large dogs chained in the back, and the dogs, probably bored out of their minds all day, had amused themselves by digging. Being a writer, I had a well-developed imagination. But even for me it was a stretch to imagine a garden emerging out of that desert of a yard.

Even though my first month in the house the weather was rainy and miserable, I made plans to achieve grace and beauty in this new landscape—somehow.

By luck, I met a landscaper who gave me a good price on building a long line of raised flower beds in a sunny corner. Another dug up the withered old bushes and a few chopped-off stumps that lined the yard. With my dwindling savings I bought some tiny juniper bushes, northern azalea, and plenty of spring flowering bulbs.

Most of the techniques of northern gardening were new to me. Father and grandmothers had all been wonderful gardeners, but in temperate and southern climates. Here in the north there were strict rules—plants did not survive below-zero temperatures unless they were "winter hardy." Luckily, everyone on my block gardened. I began to question two gardening neighbors to find out what flowers would grow in the new beds.

The first year I planted everything I could afford that was on sale at the local nursery. In an effort to cover the bare spots, I packed tiny perennial seedlings into every inch of space. But learning grace also means having a view toward future growth and allowing for it.

The first summer the flower beds looked lush and

inviting. But by the third summer the lushness had overgrown into a jungle, with the stronger plants cheerfully growing and suffocating the tiny ones. I realized I had been too shortsighted. It was expansion time. Evenings and weekends throughout that third summer found me outside digging another large bed alongside the first one and transplanting fifty plants from the original bed. They grew and grew and grew—by the next summer I had to build a third bed to accommodate all the growth.

By then I was learning to space the plants well apart to allow for their growth and beauty for many seasons to come.

Ironically, that was the year my husband and I decided to sell that house and move further out of the city. I had to say good-bye to all my flower beds, but I got to keep the lessons I had learned with them. A young couple bought the house; the wife was eager to learn about flower gardening.

In our new house, I encountered new lessons about grace and gardening. The previous owners had terraced beds in the private backyard but had not planted much in them. The first spring, as I mused over those open spaces, part of me wanted to run out and buy as many plants as the car could carry.

The other part, the wiser part, remembered all that transplanting and digging.

Poet Richard Hugo wrote about the struggle of learning, in reference to writers, which I found quite apropos to my lessons of grace and flower gardening: "Actually, the hard work you do on one poem is put in on all poems. The hard work on the first poem is responsible for the sudden ease of the second. If you just sit around waiting for the easy ones, nothing will come."

Whatever our spiritual theme in life, we will reach turning point after turning point as we practice building skills in that area. I had to work many times in those flower beds before I began to understand my particular theme: the lesson of grace.

Opening the Heart to Others

A friend told me the following story about an ECKist with a life theme of learning how to share his heart with others.

Jim (not his real name) was intelligent and insightful, but he had a reluctance to get involved in other people's lives. This had given him freedom for many years, but now he was older and lonely. The isolating wall he had carefully built was hindering his next spiritual step—allowing his heart to open. Jim's story shows how he found this important theme in his spiritual turning points.

Jim's turning point was more subtle than many of the more dramatic physical challenges that many of us face, but a change of heart can be just as hard to face.

Jim worked in an engineering plant in Dallas, Texas. Every morning he saw the same group of people get off the bus at his stop, and after a few weeks he realized these people worked in a sheltered workshop down the street. The workshop employed the mentally disabled.

One member of the group was a large woman with short red hair who appeared to have Down's syndrome. She was always terrified to cross the street.

She would stand with her shoulders hunched, fear on her face, until one of her friends would take her arm. The friend would lead the red-haired woman across the street to safety. Jim often watched this process, worrying that the small group wouldn't make it across. Traffic rushed by; the street was very busy, with three lanes in each direction.

One day Jim reached his office about forty-five minutes later than usual and saw a woman, obviously very upset, walking toward the lobby.

She seemed familiar, but Jim was late and didn't want to get involved with someone else's problems. So he went through the lobby and down the hall to his office.

In the time it took him to walk through the building, Jim realized that the woman in the lobby was the red-haired woman who had such trouble crossing the street. Shamed by his own indifference, Jim raced back to the lobby to see if he could offer his services, however belatedly. But the receptionist had already called the woman's supervisor and he was coming to escort her.

Jim gave himself a C- for the episode. He hadn't been able to overcome his spiritual inertia in time to reach out and help a fellow Soul in distress. He felt he had not made the most of that learning experience.

But opportunity always knocks again with our spiritual themes.

Two months later, Jim was again late for work. As he rounded the corner from the parking lot, he caught sight of the red-haired woman. This time it looked as if she was in real trouble. She had tried to cross the busy six-lane street alone, but the task proved impossible for her.

She stood frozen on the median, panic-stricken and hysterical.

As fast as his legs could carry him, Jim reached the woman. She grabbed his arm. "Let me help you across," he said.

"Do you know how to cross this street?" the woman asked nervously.

"Yes," Jim said, "I cross it every day, sometimes two or three times." The woman looked reassured. When the traffic cleared, the pair walked across the street, calmly reaching the other side, although the woman never let go her iron grip on Jim's arm. The woman thanked Jim, her confidence restored, and they parted.

Jim saw the woman one more time after that— she was crossing the street alone and reached the other side safely, all by herself. He realized in challenging his own personal fear of getting involved with others, he may have helped make the world a better place for one person.

Finding Options to Anger

Reviewing our past is an easy way to learn to recognize the themes running through our turning points. A friend told me about a turning point that was very difficult, since it forced her to alter a fundamental part of her behavior. Looking back on all that happened, she realized how much happier she is now because of the change.

Margaret's story could be that of any one of us. It had to do with her temper, her best defense against the world.

Raised in a crowded city that was known for its high crime rate, Margaret had always felt proud of her ability to protect herself under any circumstances. With her quick tongue, she could lash out scathingly at any potential attacker, whether it was a clerk trying to cheat her in the supermarket or someone harassing her on the subway.

In her late thirties Margaret and her husband moved to a small town in the Midwest, where Margaret got her present job working as the office manager in a small law firm.

After about six months on the job, her boss called her in one afternoon. He explained that several of the lawyers were taking offense at her quick temper and found her extremely hard to work with.

Margaret was sincerely surprised and quite hurt by her boss's comments. Growing up where anger was a convenient and popular weapon against crowded conditions, she thought little of her quickness to strike back when she felt taken advantage of. How did other people survive without this kind of defense?

Since she loved her job and times were hard, she swallowed the retorts she wanted to toss at her boss and promised to try harder to keep a lid on her temper around the office.

This was her turning point—as she said later. Life was asking her to do something differently.

Margaret began an earnest search among her friends to find people she considered good survivalists but who didn't use anger indiscriminately. One woman in her church study group seemed a perfect example, and Margaret vowed to get to know her better. Surprisingly Jeannine called her up the following weekend to go to a show at the art museum.

Jeannine was quite understanding when Margaret explained her situation. "I feel like this is an important step for me," said Margaret, "but I'm very scared to change my ways and let go of anger. It's the best defense I know, and I don't believe I have other tools to protect myself."

"Maybe your situation has changed," Jeannine offered. "I also used to live in a big city. I taught at an inner-city school, and I felt anger was the best defense against the bullies there. But when I moved here, I realized anger was a tool I no longer needed. "In fact," she added, "it stood in my way spiritually."

"But how did you let go of it?" Margaret asked.

"First I asked Divine Spirit for help in whatever way I could understand. My husband was a big help to me in this because he is very sensitive to anger; sometimes it even makes him sick. So I had to curb my instincts to lash out at him or the kids I work with whenever I felt threatened. I tried to go off by myself and cool down. I also had good friends to talk to. This showed me how to replace the anger in my life with love."

Margaret felt that the meeting with her boss and the conversation with Jeannine opened a new door. She didn't know it at the time, but she was preparing inwardly for a new step spiritually.

Life had placed the crossroads before her as a test to see what she would do. Her willingness to learn another way of being, to put anger aside, softened her heart.

The following year at an ECKANKAR seminar Margaret got real confirmation of the changes she had allowed to happen.

She was asked to give a short presentation about spiritual lessons and spoke very humbly and simply of the changes she had encountered that year. A woman she had known before came up to her in the hallway after the talk. The woman had tears in her eyes.

"I can't believe how much you've changed. How have you managed to become such a loving person in so little time? When I knew you back in the city, you had such a hard edge," the woman told Margaret.

"I listened. I did something differently, took a chance at change. And I worked hard to learn how," said Margaret.

Margaret realized that her theme of using anger had served her for many years but she had grown to the point where she needed new tools. She now watches for opportunities to use love instead of anger in situations.

Margaret shared an exercise she now uses to recognize the themes of the turning points in her life. This exercise helps her cultivate a feeling of gratitude for the lessons and experiences given to her.

If you'd like to try it, find a quiet place to be alone for fifteen or twenty minutes. You'll need your journal and pen.

☀ Exercise: Gratitude and Trust

Write down all the negative feelings you may have about yourself and your abilities, in any areas you can think of.

Imagine you are just letting all the negativity in your life flow out on the paper. Try not to censor yourself—no one but you will see this page. When you run out of things to write, take a clean sheet of paper.

Now write down all the gifts you have received from life.

You can start small at first; include even things you may take for granted like your ability to breathe, run, eat, or even to smile at someone else. Move on to bigger items that enhance your life. Take a third page. Write down what you hope to learn from life. You can divide the page into different areas, such as spiritual, work or career, family, finances, creativity, etc.

To carry this exercise one step further, get a colored highlighting marker. Highlight any parallels you see between the three sections you wrote—the things you dislike, the things you are grateful for, and the things you wish to learn.

These parallels may be your personal themes and may help you locate turning points that need looking at.

In future chapters we'll look at the real reason for seemingly negative turning points—and how to turn them into positive lessons.

But first we'll look at how to put together a spiritual toolbox to understand and work with turning points.

4. Building Your Toolbox: Dreams and Spiritual Exercises

What if someone were to hand you a toolbox that had everything in it you needed to handle turning points?

People who ride easily through turning points always seemed to me to have such a toolbox. Change would stymie them for a day—a week at the most—then they would almost visibly shake themselves and use a spiritual tool to get on with life.

I noticed these people usually spend a certain portion of their lives developing spiritual stamina. They actually practice—usually every day—the higher viewpoint of Soul.

In each of the exercises you've done so far in this book, you've actually been practicing something called a spiritual exercise. In ECKANKAR, we practice exercises like this for twenty minutes daily to learn how to use the faculty of imagination and the seeing quality of Soul to travel in the inner worlds.

Doing this each day is an excellent way to strengthen the ability to maintain a higher level of perception at any time.

41

In the following example I was able to gain this higher viewpoint in a difficult situation with a close friend only because I had put much time and love into daily practice of the spiritual exercises. Combined with a timely dream, they gave me the higher vision I needed to help her—and myself—through a dark time.

Gift of Higher Vision

A close friend was going through a lot of major changes in her life and had effectively shut herself off from the people around her. This was difficult for me, however, because she and I had just talked about how close we wanted to become. Both of us were in our thirties, without many local friends, and we wanted to spend more time together. When my friend's crisis hit, I thought naturally she would turn to me.

But she didn't. No amount of talking could reach her.

I stewed about this situation for days. When I closed my eyes to do my daily spiritual exercise, all I could see was my friend's face. I felt such sorrow and lack of understanding about what was happening. I also knew that I was caught in a morass of emotion about the situation, and before a higher viewpoint could come, I would have to free myself of the morass.

By the end of the week, I was sick of the anger and pain I felt. Before going to sleep that night I tried the exercise in chapter 1, the one with the room of fear.

I made my inner room not only filled with fog but also imagined a coating of molasses all over the floor and walls—which represented the pain I felt. It was indeed gooey and thick like molasses.

In the exercise I imagined first vacuuming out the fog of fear, then sending in a team of "spiritual" cleaners to hose down both walls and floor. The thick molasses ran out into the street. It took quite a bit of time before I felt the room was clean of all the traces of this strong emotion.

At the end of the exercise, I checked my feelings about my friend. Surprisingly most of the heavy emotion was gone. I felt much lighter. I asked Divine Spirit for any further insight that would help me understand my friend's situation, then I went to sleep.

A lovely dream came. In the dream I was visiting my friend's house. She had two vacuum cleaners going, and she was racing around the house trying to clean huge piles of dirt. She hugged me but said she didn't have time to visit. Would I please come back later when she had finished cleaning the house? She thought it would take her about a week, no longer.

When I awoke I knew the dream had given me both reassurance and an important message: My friend was cleaning out something in her inner worlds and couldn't be there for me right now. I relaxed, finally able to see the situation from a higher viewpoint.

Just as the dream had shown, within a week my friend was back—thanking me for giving her space during that difficult time.

Spiritual Workout

We work our physical muscles to get flexibility and strength; it makes sense that our inner muscles

43

also need a regular workout. As we tone these inner muscles through the daily practice of spiritual exercise, they get stronger, able to lift more and propel us more quickly into the higher viewpoint of Soul.

What is spiritual exercise?

It's simply a way to practice letting God work through us in every detail of our lives. During a spiritual exercise, we let go of the world and our worries, and listen to God. From the outside a spiritual exercise may look a lot like just sitting still, but inside it is much more active.

Mechanics of Spiritual Exercise

Doing a spiritual exercise is easy. I make up my own as needed or choose one from Sri Harold Klemp's *The Spiritual Exercises of ECK*. Soul is a creative entity, and each Soul approaches God in a different way. Some like to use visualization, others work with sound, others just have a feeling of upliftment.

As long as you follow two basic guidelines, you will have success. The first is to do the exercises each and every day. The second is to do them for twenty minutes at a time.

If you do not continue with your spiritual exercises, you may not notice a difference at first. Things will go pretty much as usual, but then you may start finding that life is slightly more difficult to deal with. While you were doing your exercises, you were tapping into a strong source of higher awareness. When you stop the regular spiritual exercises, you pull the plug and slowly lose this source of nourishment.

I had followed this rule for many years—about ten—without knowing why. It made sense. But then, like everything else, it was something I had to test for myself.

It was natural to stop doing my exercises one summer; I had just moved and there was so much to do. The first few days I hardly noticed that I didn't set aside twenty minutes each morning; I just woke up and began unpacking boxes.

After a week of not doing the exercises, things started to become hard for me.

I was short-tempered with others, less forgiving of myself. It was hard for me to be detached from my stronger emotions. I put the blame on everyone else but myself.

My two cats were the ones who got me back on track.

They loved doing the exercises each morning; they'd often curl up on my lap as I sat there. While the living room was in boxes, our favorite chair was not available, but still they sat hopefully next to it each morning at the right time.

On the sixth day the contemplation chair was finally unearthed, and my cats happily curled up at the appropriate time. Then they just stayed there.

I was still unpacking, but in a distracted and inefficient way, feeling worse about my life, my new home, everything. Walking through the living room, I finally noticed the cats. Everything hit at once.

It took me a few days to begin enjoying the exercises again. At first I was restless, not really sure why I was doing them, but the cats were solid weights on my lap so I stayed. Slowly the rhythm came back.

I began to notice the inner peace I had enjoyed before. I was convinced again.

This time, thanks to my brief lesson about the importance of the spiritual exercises and a regular schedule, I began doing them out of love rather than duty.

I wanted the state of consciousness that came with them. So I did them every day. It was that simple.

I also experimented with how long to do this daily exercise. I found that ten or fifteen minutes only got me to the point where I was relaxed and ready to receive, like tuning in a radio. Thirty minutes left me groggy. Twenty was just enough. Now I set a kitchen timer to ring at twenty minutes, so I don't have to think about the time.

Tangible Benefits

The qualities of Soul shine through all the over-coats into our physical life as we practice these spiritual exercises. Most of the time I find flexibility, love, spontaneity, and generosity are part of my life—naturally.

I am able to maintain a broader focus and perspective. And I can pay attention to my own turning points a lot better.

The desire to practice spiritual exercises regularly is not something that can be imposed on us by another person; the love for doing them has to come from within. I know people who follow the routines of their church out of duty rather than love; as a result they can be mean-spirited and have great difficulty handling change.

Spiritual growth must come from within us, rather than be imposed on us by other people or events.

Types of Spiritual Exercises

The three types of spiritual exercises I use most often are *contemplation* techniques, *visualization* techniques, and *imaginative* techniques.

Contemplation techniques are mostly listening exercises. I chant or sing a sacred word, quiet myself, give over my problem, then sit and listen.

Visualization techniques work on the principle that we, as Soul, move where we focus our attention. I often visualize the Light and Sound of God streaming in, healing and uplifting me.

Imaginative techniques use all the senses: smell, sight, sound, touch, and taste. I might imagine myself on a lakeshore. A sailboat arrives with the Mahanta, my spiritual guide, at the tiller. I touch his hand, I feel the boat rocking, and I smell the wind.

The purpose of a spiritual exercise is to create a safe place for Soul to operate freely. Whichever type of spiritual exercise gives you a feeling of peace and an open heart is the right one for you. I tuck safe places into my memory—a creek I sat by as a child, a room full of plants at the Minnesota Landscape Arboretum, a waterfall in Hawaii—and use them in my exercises to bring the sense of peace I need for my heart to open. Over the years, I've found three important keys which nurture the love and desire to keep spiritual exercise as an important part of my life.

The first key was to develop a spiritual exercise routine. The second was to learn to work with the spiritual exercises to clear out inner obstacles. The third was to find my own secret word.

Spiritual Exercise Routine

When I first began doing daily spiritual exercises in 1975, I was just putting in time. I sat for twenty minutes each morning, eyes closed and breath even. Not much happened that I was aware of. Sometimes a short flash of color would appear before my eyes. Sometimes I would fall asleep briefly and wake up marvelously refreshed.

But never did I have incredible experiences others raved about—like being outside of my body, floating on the ceiling, or consciously visiting other worlds.

Two years went by, and one afternoon I was talking to a friend who had practiced the exercises much longer than I had.

I hesitantly asked her what hers were like. Did she have the extraordinary experiences I had read about? She said no, she didn't.

I asked her why she had continued to do them if nothing had happened.

She simply explained that the reasons for doing regular spiritual exercises were more subtle for her. Many wonderful changes in her life had come about, and she saw this growth as the main benefit of her practice. Who cared about floating on the ceiling when one could have inner peace or an ability to deal with conflict better?

"Look at how you've changed," she added, turning to me.

She had known me at the beginning. To her, I was now a different person.

How Spiritual Exercises
Help with Turning Points

Why start a spiritual exercise routine? Here's one reason: as a daily problem solver. If you go into a spiritual exercise with a question, it will often be answered.

Training yourself to hear the answer takes time—and discipline. The outer ears are not easily tuned to the whisperings of Divine Spirit. But day after day of practicing the spiritual exercises will tune the inner hearing.

By the way, I recommend testing the information and ideas you get in your spiritual exercises before acting on them—that is, until you develop a sure link with Divine Spirit. You must be certain where your answers are coming from. I found that in the beginning I would misinterpret what I heard, and the results would come out skewed.

Start small in testing the answers you get. Maybe you'd ask what to have for breakfast to be your best that day. If an image comes, try it for a day and see if it helps.

You start with small questions then work up to bigger ones. See chapter 6 for more information on how to listen to the inner guidance.

Both big and little questions can be tackled in the following exercise, "Asking a Question."

Exercise: Asking a Question

Close your eyes, and take several deep breaths to relax the body.

Visualize a very peaceful setting to relax the mind. I often imagine I am standing on the porch of the boathouse at my grandmother's summer camp in the mountains. I am watching rain on the lake, but under the porch roof it is dry and comfortable. The rain makes hissing noises as it hits the surface of the water.

Use your own setting. In a relaxed way, get into some scene that will make you loosen your mental grip. This will allow images from a higher level to come through.

Now lightly place your attention on your question. Don't force your thoughts to go in any one direction, just let them ramble.

Some unexpected image or feeling or insight may pop into your consciousness. At first, when this happens, you will have a tendency to disregard it or say to yourself, "How strange!" Practice a gentle acceptance of these fleeting messages. Don't judge them at this point.

When you come out of contemplation, take a minute to write down what you saw, heard, or felt—no matter how unusual it seems. If you'd like, pay attention to whether an image repeats during the day.

Often when trying this exercise, I get very wonderful and unexpected answers to questions.

Clearing Out Inner Obstacles

Two main obstacles to benefiting from the spiritual exercises are inside us: our emotions and mind. If I sit down with strong feelings or mental worries, I cannot achieve an open heart. I end up feeling like a hamster racing around on a wheel.

But how do we clear out these inner obstacles?

One morning not long ago I was feeling very sensitive to emotional currents around me. My husband was a bit under the weather and had been very quiet all week. If I'm in a stable, balanced place this doesn't shake me, but this time it was awful. When I sat down to do my spiritual exercise, I knew the extreme sensitivity of my emotions would disrupt whatever I wanted to use the time for.

So I decided my first task was to remove the obstacles standing between me and hearing the clear voice of the Holy Spirit.

First I used the exercise in chapter 1, the fear room. I knew behind my extreme sensitivity lay a certain amount of fear that other people's states could and would upset my own balance. Then I relaxed and inwardly asked, "What next?"

The answer that came was surprising: "Reduce the amount of electrical current."

Immediately in my inner vision I saw a room surrounded by arcing blue electricity. It was arcing out of control. Out of range of the arcs, on the wall, was a dimmer switch, similar to those used for ordinary lighting. I got a second nudge: "Turn down the dimmer switch."

As I did this, the arcs of blue subsided.

The palpable tension that had been in the air was gone. I came out of my spiritual exercise feeling optimistic that the sensitivity would be calmed as well.

And it was. That day was the best I had had in a week.

Finding a Secret Word

In many spiritual practices, students are encouraged to sing or chant a sacred word. It can be the name of a saint, God, or even Amen. A favorite of mine is HU, a sacred name of God. The idea is that the word becomes a focus for the attention, something higher than oneself.

It helps spiritualize the consciousness.

Members of ECKANKAR receive a secret word with each initiation. The word, to my mind, is an empty vessel when first received. It doesn't mean much in itself. But as I begin to use it in my spiritual exercises, the word takes on power and life, like a battery being charged.

Every now and then, I'd find a word's power was diminished. At first I'd just notice I didn't get the usual lift of heart when I sang or chanted it. There wasn't much there.

At those times, I'd use a universal word, such as HU. I'd wait until Divine Spirit brought me another word.

The word would often come as a sound or image during contemplation. Once it was the name of a popular brand of cat food! I could never predict what the word would be, but when I began testing the new word, it would always make me feel uplifted, good, and balanced. It worked for a day, a week, a month, or several years. Then I would feel it had lost its charge; I would ask for and get a new one.

Using a secret word is a fine way to heighten the inner awareness, something that is very necessary when working with turning points. It becomes a vital tool in your spiritual toolbox and a great aid with the spiritual exercises.

In the next chapter we'll explore how qualities like detachment, serenity, love, and joy come from working more closely with God's will in our turning points.

5. Being a Vehicle for God

One way to work more effectively with turning points is to live from the highest state possible. In ECKANKAR, this is called being a vehicle for God.

I've tried to be a vehicle for God. But the desire to have things go a certain way—my way—has made me stumble often.

It is said that desire is the root of all pain. I believe this is referring to anything that has such a gripping hold on the heart that it won't let go until it's satisfied. When my goal is to work with the ECK, the Holy Spirit, on my turning points, strong desires can act as distracting noise and keep me from hearing God's subtle directions.

The element of desire I find hardest to live with is inflexibility.

Once a desire is set, my mind locks in and it seems impossible for me to be neutral or detached. It feels impossible to place an outcome in the hands of Divine Spirit, no matter how many spiritual exercises I do or how much I talk about detachment.

I've learned the hard way to have preferences rather than desires. Preferences are gentle requests of God, without the inflexibility of a desire.

I prefer that something happen, but I have learned by now that Divine Spirit has a much broader vision than I do. I can imagine an outcome and state my preference for it—"I'd like this job"—but I do not fuss and whine if it doesn't take place.

Who knows? I might get an even better one.

Dreaming the Highest Dream

The process is not easy, because you have to work very intentionally with preferences rather than desires. You have to be willing to let go of the outcome. A good example came two years ago, when my husband and I decided to sell our home.

For four years, we had lived in a small but comfortable house about forty minutes away from the office. Since we both worked at the same place, we could commute together. The drive was pleasant, but every now and then my husband would talk about selling our house and moving closer.

In my heart, I didn't want to move.

This home had been my first solo purchase, one that I had made before our marriage. I had poured so much love, time, and money into our present home. I imagined growing old there.

My pride and joy was my flower garden which stretched the length of our driveway and along the street. Enlarging it a little each year, I had carefully chosen perennials that flowered in contrasting colors to create a beautiful array from June to September. It was a bright spot in the neighborhood, one that made passersby stop and comment.

In the fall of our fourth year in the house I planted two hundred spring-flowering bulbs in patches around the house. It would be beautiful in May, I imagined, loving my home and garden even more.

In January my husband suggested we think more seriously about moving. In my mind's eye I saw the two hundred blooming daffodils and tulips waving in the May breeze.

It was too much. I burst into tears.

It was a stormy weekend. At night, I tossed and turned, mentally walking through my gardens, grieving over each flower. By Sunday night, just to get some sleep, I did a special spiritual exercise.

I asked the Mahanta, my inner guide, to help me say good-bye to the house. He led the way through my gardens in full summer bloom, and I said good-bye to each lily and spring bulb.

The next morning, I felt more positive. Following a nudge, I began writing a list of all the things I could possibly want in a new home. My imagination ran wild as I described a terraced garden, with plants cascading down to an enclosed lawn or patio, like a Mediterranean villa. I also wrote that I'd like to see my present garden in bloom one last summer or take part of it with me to the new house.

My husband called a real estate agent. The agent reasoned that the house could take as much as three or four months to sell. No need to look for a new house until we had a firm offer.

Four days later our plans changed.

The agent called, surprised. "There are possibly two offers on your house." Our For Sale sign wasn't even up.

"One couple is very serious," he said. "Your pictures sold them." On an impulse, I had left an album of summer garden photographs on the kitchen table.

Our house sold the next day. We were grateful, but the gratitude was tinged with panic. What if we couldn't find a new place we liked? My husband reassured me: "Look how fast our house sold! That was a miracle. The perfect house is just waiting for us."

Manifesting the Dream

We arranged to go house-hunting the next morning, but the agent only had two homes to show us. A sudden plummet in interest rates had made more houses available in our price range, but the neighborhood near work was still very expensive. I came back to the office depressed; neither home we had seen was half as nice as what we were leaving.

That afternoon I talked about our problem with a coworker.

"Oh, I just saw a lovely house that's going up for sale," she said. She described the size and price of the home, the large two-car garage, the backyard. "It was under snow, so I couldn't see what they had done out back, but it's lovely inside," she added.

I felt a tingle of excitement. "Where is it?"

"About a mile from here." She gave me sketchy directions.

I called our agent first thing the next morning. "There's a house down the road that looks good; it's in our price range," I said. "I don't know the street number. Can you look it up in your computer and arrange for us to see it?"

"Nothing's listed in the area," he said after a moment. "If it's really for sale, it'll show up soon. I'll call you."

I tried not to get my hopes up. The ECK would take care of it. We felt tremendous pressure to find a place fast, but I reminded myself that Divine Spirit had guided us this far.

That same day I went to lunch with a girlfriend. As we drove down through a residential section by the office on the way to a restaurant, we passed an attractive house that had often caught my eye. "Stop!" I yelled. A car from a local real estate company was in the driveway. A woman I took to be a real estate agent was putting a lock box for a key on the house. This must be the home for sale! I could hardly believe it.

Running up to the woman, I asked, "Is this house for sale?"

"Yes," she said. "It's just going on the market this week. The family was unexpectedly transferred back east, and they have to sell in a hurry." I arranged to see it the next morning.

That night I had a dream. In the dream I was walking through a beautifully remodeled home that was full of light. The living room was trimmed in teal blue, the floors were gleaming hardwood. Best of all was the summer garden out back. Could this be our house? I scribbled down the dream on awakening.

When we walked into the house the next morning, I couldn't believe my eyes.

Teal blue trim edged the living room; and there were the gleaming hardwood floors. It was my dream house. Although the backyard was covered in snowdrifts, on the kitchen counter were six snapshots showing a terraced garden waiting to be planted. My wish-list garden come to life!

59

I made one of the fastest decisions of my life. Moving into the living room where my husband and our agent sat talking, I said, "This house is going to go fast. We need to put an offer on it today, now." They looked at me in surprise.

"This is my dream house," I explained, telling them about my dream.

Our agent had never heard of someone buying a home based on a dream. My husband, however, knew me well enough to agree to the idea. We signed papers and a check.

Sensing that there would be competition for the house, I suggested offering more than the asking price. The agent called us later that evening to say that there was one other very interested couple, and the sellers would make a decision the next day.

Learning True Surrender

That night I had trouble getting to sleep. "It's the perfect house, your dream house. It would be so terrible if the sellers didn't choose you," my mind worried. "It's in your price range. And think of that garden."

But I knew it was in the hands of the ECK. We had followed our spiritual guidance each step of the way, down to offering more than the asking price. It was now out of our hands.

The agent called us off and on all the next morning as the owners met with their agent and tried to decide who to sell to. "It looks good," he'd say, "your income is more stable." "Not so good," he'd call back the next hour, "you have another house being sold. They're worried that deal might fall through."

60

By noon, we were nervous wrecks. I made lunch and sat at the kitchen table across from my husband, pretending to read a magazine. The phone rang; we both jumped. It was our agent again.

"You better sit down!" he said. "You got the house!"

We moved into our new house the week before my birthday. *It is quite a birthday gift,* I thought, as I watched the snow melt and a few plants come up in the flower beds. Best of all, as part of our selling agreement, the buyers of our old home let me come back one day in May and dig up a carload of perennials for my new garden.

We've been in the new house for over a year. When I look back on all the things that could've gone wrong in the sale and move, I shudder. The entire experience was an exercise for me in surrendering my personal desires.

Two Approaches

Two approaches have appeared in my life to teach me about surrender, and both have to do with goal setting.

With the first approach I set a goal for something where I am serving the self's interests, such as "I want to sell an article to this magazine." It's a narrow vision that works for a while. Then it stops working, because the goal is too limited.

If I catch on soon enough, I switch to the second approach, where I surrender my initial desire and realize that the experience is the real goal and the rest is incidental. For example, my goal becomes "I want to be a better writer so I can be of service." I become more open to receiving the gifts of the ECK in whatever form they take, not just in the limited form I can see at the time.

This attitude always brings me the greatest good, but it has not been an easy one to learn.

Inner Direction for Truer Goals

The best way I've found to set goals is from the inside out, something a friend calls "envisioning." He does a spiritual exercise where he tries to get in touch with the highest point of view.

From this Soul viewpoint he envisions a quality, a state of being, such as serenity, peace, fulfillment, courage, love. These are his true goals, the inner states he is trying to achieve. Then he visualizes the natural outer results of those inner states.

To list outer situations that would be reflections of these inner states, he uses one page in his journal for physical, another for emotional, a third for mental, and a fourth for spiritual. Each is equally important.

When I tried his exercise, I found myself quite surprised by the "goals" I wrote in each category.

From this higher viewpoint, I suddenly realized that making a lot of money has never been an end in itself for me. It's important to be comfortable, but just having money is not my purpose in this life. I certainly don't want money at the expense of more intangible goals, such as a fulfilling marriage or satisfying, purposeful work. This was a truth I had overlooked.

A Special Writing Class

When I applied my friend's exercise to my free-lance writing career, it totally changed what I was willing to do to achieve the next outer goal I had— to get published in the higher-paying magazines.

I realized what I really wanted in terms of my work life was not more fame; I actually desired to learn more courage and honesty in my writing. I wanted to overcome the barriers of fear that stood in my way. This was more important than getting my byline on those glossy pages. If fame and fortune came as a result of overcoming fears, so be it. But those were no longer the primary motives.

This realization brought a strong wave of freedom rushing through me. I relaxed inside. It was wonderful. I totally trusted life to bring me whatever was needed to achieve my inner vision of myself as a courageous, honest writer.

And life brought it in a very unexpected way.

About three months later, when I had totally forgotten the exercise I had done, I got a call from Laurence, a friend from England. He was visiting the United States for the summer and was taking a writing course from a university in my city.

Laurence was very excited. Could we get together so he could tell me about this class he was taking?

Laurence's story was to be a mirror of my own. He had asked a friend to sign him up for a summer creative-writing class. He hoped to learn how to incorporate spiritual principles into fiction stories. But instead she had registered him in a course that taught how to sell nonfiction articles to magazines. The first evening, he was surprised and slightly disappointed that the content was to be so different from what he had anticipated. But something inside urged him to stay.

The writing teacher proved to be one of the best he had ever met. She had published hundreds of magazine articles on a multitude of topics, including some esoteric ones. She had also authored at least one book and was writing a magazine column.

As she put the students through their paces, those that stayed learned the fine art of querying magazine editors and composing copy that really touched the reader.

As a result of that class, Laurence sold his first article to a large U.S. magazine. He was able to research a spiritual subject—dreams—and include interviews with experts in the field. He was also able to include his own spiritual experiences with dreams, including several exercises he loved.

I was impressed with what Laurence had accomplished and decided to try the course myself.

I wondered what I could get out of the class, but it seemed to fit my new goal of learning courage and honesty in my writing. After the first meeting, I realized why. This class would be tough. But it would also be the vehicle to teach me what I needed to learn about courage *and* allow me to break into the higher-paying magazine markets.

Within six months I had sold twelve articles, most to magazines I had been afraid to contact before the class.

The instructor and I became friends, and at her urging I joined a national organization for magazine writers, which brought me two more writing assignments. A year later, when I looked back at the goals and dreams I had written down from the envisioning exercise, I had to laugh. Life had brought me exactly the turning points I had asked for.

Working from the inside out, I had reached the inner dream of more courage and honesty in my writing. I had also gotten the outer results.

I use the envisioning exercise on an ongoing basis to set new goals for myself and review past ones. It's also a simple way of ridding myself, layer by layer, of old useless beliefs. Practicing this exercise helps me realize how much of a vehicle for God I can be through the turning points in my life—if I take the initiative.

The exercise starts with a simple contemplation to open the heart, then moves on to envisioning. If you'd like to try it, find a quiet place to be alone for twenty or thirty minutes, and take your journal with you.

☀ Exercise: Spiritual Goal Setting

First, close your eyes. Relax as thoroughly as you can. Set aside all your worries, concerns, and problems for this period of time—you can come back to them in half an hour.

Now imagine a person, animal, place, or object that you love more than you have ever loved anyone or anything.

Focus on that feeling of intense love—it can be in your past or present. Feel the love roll through you in great waves.

Now take the object of your love out of your vision. Just feel the love itself. This love is very pure. It has no object, no desire to change anything. It just loves. There is a great feeling of peace that comes with it because no action, decision, or movement is necessary. You feel safety and great well-being, as if all is right with your world.

When you feel this love flowing out of you and you feel refreshed by it, open your eyes.

Turn to a fresh page in your journal. You'll be evaluating an area of your life that you'd like to infuse with this high level of love and well-being. It can be physical health, finances, a relationship, a friendship, family, emotions, mental learning, spiritual advancement, or whatever you have a nudge to improve.

First write a short paragraph or a few sentences answering this question: How do I see this area of my life now?

Second, start a new paragraph, and answer this question: How would this area of my life look if it was filled with this higher well-being and love?

Third, write the answer to this question: What actions can I take to bring this about? List one or several things that come to you, even if they seem silly or irrelevant. Have any signs appeared lately that might give you clues as to what actions to take?

Fourth, look at what you must surrender to bring this about.

What old beliefs or attitudes about yourself or your life could be tossed out now (like my belief that I must become a millionaire)? What must be changed to fit your new vision?

You can do this each day for a different area in your life, even making finer distinctions within categories.

Whenever I work through this envisioning exercise, I put the notes away then look at them six months later. Just as my desire to become a better writer brought me the special writing class, life inevitably brings me a way to break through the limits that are holding back the well-being I want in any area of my life.

I have found that consciously deciding to be a vehicle for the higher good makes my turning points slight shifts on the road rather than bumpy potholes and sharp curves.

In the next chapter we'll explore a way to get good guidance along the way.

6. Inner Guidance— Learning to Listen

When I was four years old, I spent most of my weekday mornings at my grandmother's apartment.

She was in her sixties then, a very robust white-haired woman, with years of experience organizing people and planning projects. Each morning she would sit for about forty minutes in silence, often with her eyes closed, sometimes jotting notes in a small black binder she kept close by.

My mother explained this was how Grandmother got her spiritual guidance. This was her quiet time, when she listened to God's instructions for her that day.

When pressed once, she explained the process to me: She'd simply think about a topic or a problem, letting it loosely roll around in her mind, and suddenly "guidance" would come. It was often no more than a subtle feeling to do this or that: often an idea that she had not even considered would float into her mind. She believed sincerely that the guidance was celestial; she had no doubt in herself as being worthy of this kind of special attention from the Divine.

Grandmother was very good at recognizing turning points before they arrived.

She'd get hunches or feelings about some event or decision. She'd wait until the time felt right to act or speak. She'd ask for counsel but always make the final decision after a brief moment of silent "guidance" or an overnight sleep.

I realize now the early tutoring I had in recognizing the inner guidance all around me—Grandmother lived and breathed according to this guidance.

Tuning Your Inner Ears

Developing a sense of inner guidance is a good first step to awareness of personal turning points. You get better at listening by practicing the Spiritual Exercises of ECK every day.

But exactly how does inner direction come to a person? What are the ways you can develop more of this inner sensitivity?

First, inner guidance is not the same for everybody. Some get nudges; others get images, a sound, or a subtle feeling. Just as there are hundreds of radio stations available to listen to, each of us has the ability to listen and receive our own individual guidance, by tuning to the constant broadcast on our very own twenty-four-hour radio station. The trick is being able to tune in to the station and keep tuned. That takes practice and trust.

My friend Dave practices listening for guidance whenever a decision needs to be made, no matter how small. When I first met him I was puzzled at this.

In the middle of a story he'd stop, be silent for a minute, then say, "I guess I can't talk about that."

Pressed to explain, he'd just tell me he had gotten a queasy feeling in his gut, inner guidance that he was crossing a line he shouldn't.

I was intrigued with this and began practicing it. The inner guidance came very subtly sometimes, oftentimes very strongly. My mother would get such nudges to call me long-distance, often when I was down in spirits, just to offer her help. We used to joke about her "inner link" with family members.

I have found there are certain practices which help this tuning in and others that hinder it.

Inner guidance comes without warning, so there's little way to predict when it will come—just ways to keep the radio tuned to the right station. I practice listening during my daily spiritual exercises, which are often similar to my grandmother's quiet time. I keep a notebook handy to jot down any ideas that float through as I sing HU or another sacred word. Sometimes the ideas are unexpected answers to problems I've been stewing over. Sometimes they are as simple as a friend's name—and when I'd follow this nudge and call the friend, she would tell me how much she needed to talk just then.

Testing the Guidance You Get

As I discussed in chapter 4, it's always good to test the guidance. Small instances, like choosing one of two equally good routes to drive to work, can become the testing ground. I ask inwardly, "Which way today?" then take the road that comes to mind. Often I can find no difference between the routes, but sometimes I'd avoid accidents or construction delays that might make me late for a meeting.

The guidance comes more and more frequently as I do these little tests, listen more carefully, and use what I receive. When I ignore it out of tiredness, stress, anger, or fear, I regret my decision often enough to return to listening.

I find that guidance comes through most steadily and clearly when I am in a relaxed state and neutral in my attitude. To maintain this as much as possible, I practice my twenty minutes of spiritual exercises every day. I also record dreams and any experiences that seem significant, since they often hold clues to guidance. I now trust the process enough to scribble down meaningless dreams in the middle of the night when they wake me, only to read them later and discover that I've been visited by certain ECK Masters or taken Soul Travel journeys.

During the night, these experiences may not make much sense, but I often find their meaning at a later date.

I also pay close attention to any event or conversation that causes a strong reaction, either unexplained repugnance or attraction. If I can, I write this down. It may be inner guidance, alerting me to a future turning point.

A Story That Became Real

In the writing class I wrote about in chapter 5, the instructor asked us to bring in old photographs for a class exercise. We passed them around the circle, each person choosing one unfamiliar photo that struck a chord. I decided this would be a great way to practice inner guidance. Listening, I had a nudge to choose a tiny black-and-white picture of a solitary woman in front of a whitewashed one-room house, the prairie in the background.

We were then asked to sit quietly with the picture and begin writing whatever came to mind— whatever thoughts or images struck our fancy. A spiritual exercise on inner listening, indeed.

I began to write a story of an elderly woman standing in front of her house in the last summer of her life.

She was a creative person but hampered by convention in the city. Her mother had wanted her to be a doctor, which was fairly radical in those days, but the thought of being around all that sickness repulsed her. She had been a brooding, serious girl, stiff in the company of others but joyous and carefree off by herself. Her mother had seen life in neat boxes, but as a young girl this woman had seen it in fragrant waves of color, like the autumn-tipped trees blowing wildly in the wind or the expanse of prairie she imagined was west of her coastal home.

She had found the house in the aged photograph when she ran away from home. She had traveled west and lived there for the last fifty years of her life. She saw the house as a stray puppy looking for someone to care for it, and she had plenty of time, generosity, and patience.

I was silent for a long time after reading my story to the group. Emotion had crept into my voice, and I almost began to cry.

The group marveled at how alive the woman had become for me. I realized that my years of developing an inner ability to listen carefully had allowed me to peek into a past life of my own, through the aged photo. I may not have been the woman in the picture, but through the exercise, I understood more about why I loved the prairie, solitude, and having my own house. Understandings like this have helped me meet turning points and handle them better.

Like any skill, the ability to listen to inner guidance is one that comes with practice, patience, and persistence. Below is an exercise I still use on days when I feel far from Divine Spirit and God and need my inner link strengthened.

☼ Exercise: Strengthening Inner Guidance

For a day imagine that each decision—as small as what to eat for lunch or what clothes to wear—is really important to your life's plan. Spend a second asking inwardly which breakfast food to eat, which pair of shoes to wear, which route to work to take, which chair to sit in at a meeting—and take note of the subtle images that come into your mind's eye.

If nothing comes at first, be patient and practice the exercise another day. Write down whatever results you have.

Did you receive any inner guidance? Did you follow it? What happened when you did or didn't?

By keeping a log of your progress, you may realize that you have been working with inner guidance all along.

The best way to begin to develop your awareness of inner guidance is to realize you already have it.

Just assume that you are connected as Soul to

74

the source of all creation, which is guiding you through your turning points. This doesn't mean walking around hearing voices all the time—to me, inner guidance doesn't come as a clear voice. It's more often a subtle nudge or a passing idea.

In ECKANKAR, training with inner guidance comes very directly through the Living ECK Master's discourses, books, and talks, as well as nightly instruction in the dream state. You can also work on seeing life from a higher viewpoint and with greater awareness of inner guidance by putting attention on your dreams and spiritual experiences.

Inner Guidance through Symbols

Some people enjoy working with symbols. A friend chose the symbol of a blue feather to remind herself of inner guidance. She wanted to write a book but wasn't sure if she had the stamina or if it was the best direction for her at the time. So she made an inner pact with Divine Spirit.

She chose the blue feather as an unusual symbol, telling no one else but figuring that each time it came to her attention, it would be more than simple coincidence.

That week, blue feathers began popping up everywhere.

Standing in line in the supermarket, she noticed that the woman in front of her had blue feathers printed on her dress. A friend sent a gray-blue gull's feather with a letter that arrived that week. Walking on the beach, she found another blue feather. The collection was growing. I was enthused by her story and created the following spiritual exercise.

It can help you learn to recognize and work with turning points by creating a personal symbol to remind you to be alert.

☀ Exercise: Symbols of Turning Points

Choose a symbol that means "turning point" to you.

Make a written pact with Divine Spirit in your dream journal to recognize just how a turning point—a significant change in your life—is being announced whenever this symbol appears. Give yourself six months, and make careful notes each time you see or hear your chosen symbol.

You may come across it only once, but it may still be highly significant.

Practicing this exercise puts you on spiritual alert. It allows God to begin working with you to further develop your awareness of inner guidance. Then you can be a greater vehicle for Divine Spirit, the ECK, in your life.

In the following chapter, we'll look at why inner guidance is the first step to establishing a closer relationship with the ECK Masters.

7. Help from Spiritual Masters

If we believe that life is essentially for our spiritual benefit, then it would not be surprising to learn that Masters of life would be available to help us with our journey through it. In ECKANKAR, there are the Vairagi ECK Masters who work together under the direction of the Living ECK Master.

Many people who come to the teachings of ECK have had experiences with these Masters for many years—often since childhood.

A true spiritual Master will not try to do our work with turning points for us. Rather he or she will lend a helping hand, give inner and outer guidance, and be a beacon in the night—someone always there to remind us of the purpose of our journey when the signs get subtle or there is trouble.

I came to a crossroads several years ago where I believed I had lost my link with God. I was helped by the Living ECK Master in the dream state.

Because of the particulars of my personal crisis, the Master's help came in the guise of my grandmother, the same person who had been my mentor from early childhood in all things practical or spiritual.

To understand how my grandmother could help

me in this way, you need to know a little about her. She was a leading Presbyterian at Brown Memorial and had a unique understanding about God. She combined faith healing, bake sales, homemade sermons, and weather predictions. Her faith made her a rock in the church community and the strongest person I knew.

As I mentioned in chapter 6, I began spending weekdays with my grandmother when I was four. Mom would drop me off on the way to work each morning about seven. I would tiptoe into the apartment because Grandmother would be having her quiet time, getting her inner guidance.

Grandmother's business and life's mission was a summer hiking-and-canoeing camp for children. She never advertised; she had faith that word of mouth and God's will would bring the right children to her door. She was right too. The camp was rarely lacking for applicants, and many came back every summer of their childhood. Although we made fun of her all-purpose connection with God, we only half-scoffed when Grandmother's faith appeared to bring sunny weather and a good wind right before a sailing race.

Grandmother guided me through my growing-up years. Although she was a strict disciplinarian and had strong opinions about how things should be done, she loved me dearly. I never doubted that love.

That's why when I reached a crisis in my life, she was the one who rescued me. But the help came after she died.

A Crisis of Faith

A year before Grandmother died, Mom called cross-country one evening to tell me someone had mugged my grandmother. They had knocked her down and stolen her purse. She had lain there in the cold, hurt and frail, waiting for God to help her.

But it was an hour before anyone came.

Later she was angry. Angry someone in that safe section of town should be prey to such activity. Angry that her husband sat alone upstairs awaiting her return instead of being at her side, sheltering and protecting her. Angry, most of all, that the God she talked to each morning had let her lie helpless on the pavement.

When I saw her about a month later, fear had replaced the anger.

Her faith had been mortally shaken, and she was simply waiting to die. At the first serious doubt her faith, based on physical strength and mental ability, had shattered around her like pieces of brittle glass. Now she wondered if God really could protect her when she had nowhere else to turn.

I was to face the same doubt ten years later. Like my grandmother, I had always depended on a special connection with God. Grandmother's faith had rested on outer proof, like good weather and a full camp roster. Mine had been shored up by brilliant inner experiences and a strong sense of knowing what to do next.

Entering the Void

My faith had been untested for fifteen years. Then a turning point came. God tapped me on the shoulder when my life was at an all-time high.

The tests began slowly. At first, it was simply a feeling of losing my spiritual anchor points. I stopped remembering my dreams. Then I lost my inner guidance: I would ask God what to do and end up in a mess when I followed my inner nudge.

For a year, I watched my world change. Outwardly all was normal. Inwardly, I walked in a place totally unfamiliar to me. Like Grandmother, I struggled with the same fear that God had left me high and dry.

But there was one difference between us: Grandmother's religion had not readied her for the natural transition away from human faith to spiritual knowing.

She had no spiritual Masters to turn to. But I had the teachings of ECKANKAR.

Inwardly I asked the Living ECK Master for help. I had received so much assistance from him, through dreams and outer circumstances, in my fifteen years as an ECKist. Maybe he would send someone to help guide me through this void.

And he did.

Suddenly, after months of blackness, I began to remember a recurring dream. I would be with my grandmother, setting up for a dinner party in her apartment in some beautiful inner place.

As we placed the china and silverware along the table's edge, Grandmother would be discoursing on a lesson she had taught me as a child, like carrying through. "To carry through, dear, just concentrate. You know you can do it. Pay attention to how you're placing that dinner plate, how you put the forks on the table. Put all of yourself there, and God will be there too."

Night after night, the Living ECK Master sent me in my sleep to her apartment for instruction,

80

inspiration, and hope—all the things she had given me as a child. She soothed my troubled spirit in the mundane activities that accompanied the dream—brownie-making, dusting the piano, transplanting an African violet.

The dreams and assistance from the Living ECK Master via my grandmother lasted less than a year, and so did my doubts about God. One day I realized the doubt was gone.

During the year I had learned to recognize God in the joy I took in small tasks, like setting the table or reading a poem. I no longer desperately sought evidence that God loved me in brilliant inner experiences. Now I knew God was indeed in all of life, even in the most subtle of things.

About that time, I stopped seeing Grandmother in my dreams. Instead, one night a brief picture of her hallway appeared, accompanied by her voice from the kitchen: "This is the past. I've moved on now."

The Living ECK Master knew that the best person to get me back on my feet spiritually and through the next turning point was my grandmother. Only she could remind me of where God truly was—in the small things in life.

Not long after that, I received an invitation to take the next higher initiation in ECKANKAR, a confirmation that I had indeed passed through a doorway with the help of love.

Dream Master

One of the most common helping tools the Living ECK Master uses is the dream state. Our natural defenses against assistance—the belief that we can handle anything with willpower or the mind—are softened, and the spiritual teachings can slip in. In dreams, he appears as the Dream Master.

In a recent ECKANKAR writing workshop I led, a woman read a beautiful story about how she received help in her dreams when moving from an apartment to her first home.

The apartment had been an upper story, back-alley location; brick walls were all she saw from her windows. In her heart she felt a deep longing for greenery and open spaces, and she silently set a goal to someday live surrounded by trees and flowers.

She had noticed for some time that she was not happy with her life, but she didn't connect it to where she was living and her longing for country spaces. Still the signs were there in little things.

Finally one night she asked the Dream Master for some help.

What was wrong with her life? She didn't recall much from her dreams that night, but she woke with a wonderfully peaceful feeling. Everything would be all right.

That morning two things happened that shook her life: Her husband said he'd like to begin looking for a place in the country, and the landlord announced he was selling the apartment building to a land developer. The couple would have to find a new place right away.

The woman was frightened. She was older now, and she wasn't sure that such a change would be good for her. But remembering the peaceful feeling from her dream, she spent the day inwardly turning things over to the Living ECK Master.

And it was only a few days later that they found their new home through an ad in the newspaper.

Only fifteen minutes farther into the country, the house sat on a small lot surrounded by huge trees. After a few days of unpacking and settling in, the woman felt her life had become a wonderful thing. She realized that the move—despite her fears—was a wonderful gift from the ECK. Her husband even commented that she seemed different.

She now looked forward to coming home from work, to helping him make dinner in their tiny kitchen, and especially to spending a few moments outside looking up at the shade trees that lined the neighborhood roads.

Dream Assistance

When she told me about the experience, the woman said she was now aware of the subtle help she had received in her dream.

The turning point was a difficult one for her, but because of her faith in the Living ECK Master, it became a simple step-by-step manifestation of the preference for a new and better life she had prepared for in those years before the move.

For her, the house was a spiritual metaphor.

She was ready to make an inner as well as outer change, and the new home gave her "more freedom inside," she said. Her living quarters paralleled the new freedom she felt in her life. Just being in an open space with lawn and trees—away from the cramped quarters and brick walls—allowed her heart to open.

ECK Masters will give sincere seekers all the

tools they need to take themselves through a difficult turning point. A friend who had recently gone through a divorce told me about an exercise she had received in contemplation. She called it the Emerald City exercise because it reminded her of Dorothy and friends in *The Wizard of Oz*.

It helped her gather the tools necessary to continue her journey home.

☼ Exercise: Going to the Emerald City

Make an inner appointment before sleep or doing a spiritual exercise to go to the Emerald City.

This can be any sort of place you can imagine—but it must have the ability to polish everything about you. Like attending a fabulous health spa that tones every part of your body, you will come back from your trip to the Emerald City with your inner bodies in tip-top shape.

Before going to sleep or doing the spiritual exercise, write down an image of what you think the Emerald City might be. You might see beautiful beings combing your hair, mending your clothes, massaging your tired muscles, polishing your shoes.

Whatever would bring your bodies into health and wellness is possible here.

In the morning or after the exercise, make note in your journal about how you feel.

Life Is Always Expanding

In the television series *I'll Fly Away,* heroine Lily Harper said, "With change often comes fear of the future, the unknown. But also hope."

I wrote this down one evening when we were watching the show. Hope to me is ever-present, because I am convinced of the constant help I am given by the ECK Masters.

I also like this quote by Ray Bradbury, the famous science-fiction writer: "Living at risk is jumping off the cliff and building your wings on the way down." That's where the ECK Masters help most: giving step-by-step instruction on building wings. Life often feels like a continuous out-of-control free fall until we begin trusting that we do indeed receive the help we need. When we begin to notice that a superior consciousness is guiding our lives, we know that what is good now can only become better in the future.

But when change starts, we don't always have enough hope or trust—because we can't see where we've been compared to where we're going. Sometimes we don't know we've been living inside a room filled with stale air until we allow ourselves to step outside and take a deep breath of fresh air.

This happened to me often enough. Until I could get perspective on where I was, I fought change, kicking and screaming. Until I realized that good was indeed becoming great, change just meant fear to me.

How do we keep reminding ourselves of the ever-expanding property of life?

Down in the dumps one rainy weekend, I once wrote myself two lists: (1) everything that I was afraid could happen in my life, and (2) everything I was grateful for having now. The "afraid of" list

85

included fears both great and trivial, such as my cats being poisoned by an irate bird-loving neighbor. The "grateful" list included those who loved me, those I loved, and the bounteous aspects of my life. I put both lists away in my journal, making a note to review them in a year.

When the year was up, I read both lists. The "afraid" list made me laugh: nothing on it had happened except one item, and that change was definitely for the best. The "grateful" list had only expanded, grown more wonderful beyond my dreams.

And many points on my "grateful" list were gifts from the ECK Masters.

Living in Color

Expanding our vision is a slow process for some of us. One example is a friend I'll call Anna. Anna is a beautiful, talented woman in her midthirties who has had a series of unsuccessful relationships and marriages. They followed a very predictable pattern, but Anna was unable to see that for many years.

It wasn't until she met her present husband, Jake, that the pattern was broken. And Anna was able to gain a greater perspective and expand her vision about herself and her life.

Anna's pattern went like this: Each time she met someone who attracted her, she sparkled and shone. The man was usually dazzled and led her in a whirlwind courtship, showering her with gifts and promises of happiness. But as the golden days of romance passed and the relationship began to demand commitment and compromise, Anna would lose interest. Inside her, she could feel a deep restlessness, and unconsciously her eye began to rove, seeking the next encounter, the next relationship.

Soon after her second marriage ended, Anna met Jake.

Jake was older; he had also been through two marriages before he met Anna. He recognized her restlessness as something he had experienced also, and he was aware of what it did to relationships, since it had broken up several of his. But Jake and Anna were strongly drawn to each other, and the challenge began for both of them—to make this one last. In their hearts, both Anna and Jake were tired of the merry-go-round of romance. Also, Jake was willing to work at their relationship. He made Anna look at herself and her beliefs, and challenge them.

Anna's new perspective allowed her to move forward and change her agreement with life.

Not long after this Anna had a dream that showed her how far she had come. In the dream an ECK Master took her to stand in front of a long mirror. Jake stood beside her.

"You're not wearing black and white anymore," Jake said.

"No," said Anna, fanning out the skirt of her bright orange-red dress. "I am wearing all colors now."

Anna realized the dream meant she had moved from a state of black and white—or narrow viewpoints about life and relationships—to one of many colors, a wider vision.

How ECK Masters Teach Us

The ECK Masters teach us through dreams and also through messages in the waking state. They will often send me a not-so-subtle outer sign about my progress. It can be a series of unusual events: three wrong-number phone calls received in a day, seeing a series of red cars near my house, finding the same song on the radio each time I turn it on. These are important messages to me from the Divine, if I can decipher them.

Once when I was discouraged about my spiritual progress, I began to see yellow school buses everywhere I went. If I was on the freeway, a school bus would pull in front of me. If I was stopped at a traffic light, two or three school buses would be turning in the cross traffic. And the buses were always bright yellow.

I puzzled about this message for days. Then it hit me. School is for learning, being a student of life. The message was, "Soul (yellow color) is still learning."

Another time I had a terrible pain in my shoulder, in the trapezius muscle. I went to doctors and masseuses, but I couldn't seem to shake the pain. Finally I began to see it as an extraordinary event— a waking dream message—and deciphered it. When I thought of the word *trapezius* I immediately saw a trapeze. It was locked up and not swinging freely, as it should. I realized the tight muscle reflected an area of my life that was also locked up.

When I freed myself from the limitations, my shoulder stopped hurting.

Each person will have his or her own ideas as to what the message is. For each, it may be different. I've learned these messages are very personalized to the listener.

In the higher worlds, all good qualities exist. Pain, discomfort, negative emotions, crises, and lack of love are all a result of being out of balance with one or more spiritual laws of these higher worlds of God.

Through dreams and waking messages, the ECK Masters simply point out the law that needs to be followed, and we can adjust ourselves accordingly.

You've probably heard of physical trainers, who come to your house and lead you through a specially tailored workout session. I like to use the following exercise to set up an inner relationship with one of the ECK Masters as a personal spiritual trainer.

Spiritual trainers are helping us work our spiritual muscles every moment of our lives; often we are just not aware of the help we're being given.

Exercise: Meeting Your Spiritual Trainer

Close your eyes, relax, and quietly chant the word *HU* or another sacred word. Feel the love of God enter your heart; put your attention on whatever image will bring you more of this love.

Now say to yourself inwardly, "I am Soul. As Soul I am here to learn _____ right now," and fill in the blank.

Immediately open your eyes, and write down whatever you got.

The answer might surprise you. Realize that your mind might try to cancel out this message, so be prepared to accept the first thing that appears when you say the word *learn*.

Now close your eyes again.

89

Inwardly say to the Living ECK Master, "I would like to learn more about this. Please let's meet tonight in my dreams, and you can take me to whomever and whichever place is right for my spiritual development in this area."

Be sure to keep a record of whatever happens in your dreams.

Again, it might surprise you who you meet. Don't disregard the help if it comes in the guise of a friend or someone close to you. Remember how my grandmother assisted me in the earlier story. The ECK Masters use whatever is needed to break down the resistance of the lower bodies.

The Simplest Lesson of All

A wonderful storyteller, Mike Avery, told me this fable. It shows that no matter how wise we are, we are always learning from true masters of life who appear in many forms.

One day a muskrat who lived on the shores of the North Umpqua river read the long work of a renowned prophet. Not understanding the prophet's treatise, the muskrat undertook a long journey by foot to speak to the man.

Weary and bedraggled, the muskrat arrived on the prophet's doorstep.

"Oh, noble prophet," the muskrat said. "I would like to further understand your magnificent work. I read it, but it was way over the head of a humble one such as myself. But since I am a devotee of truth, I came to learn from you." He bowed low.

"Well," said the prophet kindly, "let's start with my

book. Did you understand anything you read?"

"Only this," said the muskrat, "that to know truth you must love something with your whole being."

The prophet stood dumbfounded. "I can teach you nothing," he said humbly, and turning, walked back inside.

The muskrat, disappointed, turned to go back home. The prophet watching his footsteps said to himself, "What a wise and noble muskrat. He said in one sentence what it took me volumes to say."

In the next chapter, we'll see how difficult turning points can be handled more easily with inner assistance.

8. Disaster or Design?
Learning from Difficult
Turning Points

A favorite writing book I discovered many years ago is Gabriele Rico's *Writing the Natural Way*. In it is a writing exercise she calls clustering.

This exercise appears in many other books under different names and is applied to different objectives. For our purposes, however, it goes like this: You start with a question or a situation you want to explore. It may be about something that's troubling you or a turning point that seems difficult to understand. You think of a word or phrase that sums it up, then write this word or phrase in the center of a clean sheet of paper.

At this point you begin to free associate and write down other words that come to mind when you think of the central word or phrase.

You draw strands out from this center. Each strand ends with a word or phrase that came into your mind as you contemplated your central word or phrase. New ideas, ways of looking at the situation, pour out.

Sometimes we get stuck in a turning point, especially

those that seem very difficult or life-altering. We really can't see which way to go, and the fear of making a mistake paralyzes us.

This exercise is a way to break free of the paralysis by letting Soul speak.

Soul, the True Self, always has an answer. The mind and emotions are sometimes so loud, Soul cannot pass this answer to the human self to be considered and acted upon. This is especially hard when the changes we face involve others or force us to face a part of ourselves. The story below is a personal example.

When I first wrote about this turning point, which involved the dramatic failure of a business I had begun, I became very ill. I ran between the bathroom and my desk as I wrote about it. I had not talked about the experience for almost five years, except with my husband and two close friends. It was just too painful.

Writing about it, especially doing the Soul traveling technique on page 98 on the lesson it brought me, began the healing.

Rico's second book, *Pain and Possibility: Writing Your Way through Personal Crisis,* talks about this: "Paradoxically, by letting go, by externalizing feelings in words, we gain a greater ability to take charge of our own lives, and begin to see the patterns within the seeming chaos." This is what happened to me.

Finding Order in the Chaos

In 1980 I met and married a man who worked as a chef in the restaurant where I waitressed. As passionate about food and cooking as I was, Eric wooed me on one of our early dates with an elabo-

94

rately garnished home-cooked meal. We had moved to Portland and both got jobs in a booming natural foods store, I as an instructor for cooking classes and Eric in the company's public relations department. Backed by plenty of company money, my classes were well advertised and quite successful.

I designed the curriculum, taught, and hired other teachers, and organized the classroom kitchens. Proud of our success, Eric and I thought having our own school would be fun, and possibly a gateway to fame and fortune.

So we packed our bags and moved south to the San Francisco area to try our luck.

Both Eric and I believed strongly in inner guidance, and in this venture the instructions were coming fast. Both of us got daily nudges, ideas, and obvious hints from Divine Spirit to talk to certain people, investigate certain locations, check certain sources of financing.

Yellow-Brick Road

The path was paved with gold—from conception to manifestation. A 1200-square-foot storefront housing the cooking school and cookware store took just under six months to open.

We poured all our time into the school. Other than three years I had had in vitamin sales, neither of us knew much of anything about business, but we believed in our idea, and the idea found backers who believed in us. On opening day, the store was flooded with people who had seen our ads and my hand-lettered flyers. We served fresh cookies and cider, gave sushi-making demonstrations in the school kitchen, held a raffle for gourmet cookware, and took in sales beyond our wildest dreams.

All the month's cooking classes filled in a week. Innocent of the changing times, neither of us could predict the recession of the early-1980s that was to begin just a year later. At opening, the school was an instant success. California is always looking for novelty, and we were in the spotlight for that time. A major U.S. newspaper ran an interview, I was featured in a syndicated food column in 46 newspapers, people flew in from as far as Switzerland to take our two-week intensive course on natural foods gourmet cooking.

The classes kept filling. Eric and I worked very long hours and began to pay back our investors. Success lasted through the end of that year; and when the year turned, it brought personal turning points.

I was beginning to discover that I still loved teaching and was passionate about food, but I hated running a full-time business. We had three employees but no bookkeeper. Neither Eric nor I had had much experience with managing cash flow or other business necessities. We knew enough to draw the first round of customers, but not enough to sustain them on the long haul.

By the beginning of the fourth year, both our marriage and the business had fallen apart.

Stress had eaten away at any foundation we had had, and we decided to go our separate ways. I paid Eric a share of the business income while I ran the day-to-day operation. Meeting Eric's payment and the small staff's salaries was about all I could manage each week, indebted to many suppliers with no way to pay.

That summer, I felt more and more trapped, looking into a future with no hope. Why hadn't it worked? Both Eric and I had listened to our spiritual guidance, had done everything right each step of the way, and had had the best of intentions. Yet, due in part to economic times, failure was imminent, beyond our control. I spent long sleepless nights, devastated by the weight on my shoulders.

A Difficult Crossroads

One August evening I went over the figures again. There really didn't seem to be any way out of the mess. I had tried every possible trick to boost sales and class attendance, offering discounts and bring-a-friend programs. It seemed as if everything was against the success of the business.

But I wanted to keep trying, not give up yet. *There must be an honorable way out of this,* I thought.

By then I had hired an accountant. He called unexpectedly that evening to discuss the books. Overwhelmed by the dead-end situation I faced, I asked him if there was anything we hadn't tried. Were there any ideas he could think of to get the business back on its feet?

"Is that what you really want?" he asked.

"No," I answered slowly, realization dawning. "I've had enough." "Then there's always bankruptcy," he said.

When he said the word, I felt the world stand still. If I had known what I know now about turning points, I would have recognized one—a big one, a life-altering one—facing me at that moment.

Everything in my being shouted no at the thought of bankruptcy. Even my spiritual understanding at

97

that time said it was wrong, a terrible choice, creating worse karma, or spiritual debt, than I could ever repay. I believed that bankruptcy did not exist in the spiritual worlds.

My accountant waited through my silence, while the thoughts were churning in my head, then quietly reminded me that this was a business decision. Emotions must be put aside. He knew a little about my spiritual beliefs and my strong sense of right and wrong, payment of debts being one of the strongest.

"These are not decisions to be made lightly," he said, "but if there is no other recourse, the physical world has provided this as a way to start fresh."

I told him I would think about it.

I sat down that night and did a turning point exercise, like the one described below. Since it was so much on my mind, in the center of my page I wrote the word *failure* and then wrote anything that came to mind around it.

⛆ Exercise: Soul Traveling through a Turning Point

Take a clean sheet of paper, and in the center write a question, phrase, or word that is the heart of your turning point as you see it.

Now close your eyes, relax, and sing HU or a sacred word to spiritualize the consciousness.

Lightly put your attention on the question, word, or phrase in the center of your page. Then write anything that comes into your mind about the question, word, or phrase, and draw lines to connect it with the center, as in the diagram below. It can be a thought, feeling, person's name, place, object, color, smell, or image—anything.

Don't censor yourself. Unexpected concepts or images may be coming from a higher place than the mind's censor. As Soul, you have access to that higher place.

Below is an example of things that might emerge as you try the exercise:

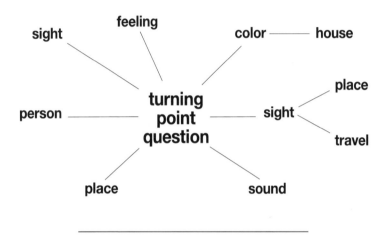

As I was doing my turning point exercise, I unearthed some very deep feelings about the decision I was about to make.

Part of me believed that Eric and I had made a mess and would need to be punished for it, to lie in the mess for a while, to suffer. Another part of me questioned this idea: "Was it all my doing? Hadn't I really done the best I knew how each step of the way?"

I also looked at why I had started the business in the first place and found I hadn't had many goals of my own—I was following Eric's lead. I wanted to share what I loved with others, but I really didn't care about doing it in my own cooking school.

I wasn't after fame, fortune, or huge success. I just wanted to make a living doing something I loved. The exercise allowed me to look at what I had learned so far.

The next step came that night in a dream.

Assessing the Karmic Balance

Doing an exercise where a turning point and its lessons are explored can be a key aspect in recognizing the purpose of more dramatic turning points.

On the surface these may look like real disasters. Often the outcome is out of your hands. Your only job is to do the best you can at that particular moment, then watch as life shifts the pieces on the chessboard in front of you and opens up new options.

As I did the exercise, a truth emerged from the turmoil of my shame and negative feelings about bankruptcy: "If I learn something important here then perhaps it is the best choice."

Four years of suffering with a failing business had taught me so much about money management. Was that really the lesson here? Could I take this new understanding of finances and live my life differently, start afresh?

I was still very unsure of what the karmic payback of this action would be. That night I had a dream.

I was standing in line at a supermarket checkout. Sri Harold Klemp, the Mahanta, the Living ECK Master, was standing next to me. The cashier had just totaled my purchases. "That comes to $400," she said. This was much more expensive than I had calculated, and I knew my bank account would be severely depleted. But even in the dream I was willing to pay whatever I owed and began writing out the check.

"Wait a minute," Sri Harold said. "I think we've been overcharged."

He pointed to an advertising coupon lying on the counter. "This coupon entitles us to a reduced price at this time. And someone else must have added these extra items to the order; we really don't want them. Shall we return them?" he asked me.

"Sure," I said.

After the cashier had corrected the bill, the total was much less. The Master and I walked out of the store with very little to carry. I felt light and free, as if a heavy burden had been lifted.

When I woke I knew immediately that the dream was significant.

For me, the number four signified the Fourth Circle of Initiation in ECKANKAR, where I was at the time. It also reflected the four years I had been in business. I felt the cashier represented the Lords of Karma, those beings that impartially dole out credits and debits for each Soul. She was ringing up the total I owed karmically from my four years of experience with the school.

At first the total was very high, an amount that would almost deplete my karmic account (my checkbook). But rather than just accept this at face value, the Living ECK Master pointed out some errors in calculation. And the amount I actually paid was far less, something I could afford at this initiation level.

It was a good sign. I felt sure the Holy Spirit, the ECK, was telling me to go ahead with the bankruptcy and trust that it was the best option.

I slept one more night on the decision, and in the morning I knew it was the only path I had the strength to take now.

I filed for bankruptcy in late summer.

Paying Back the Debt

Despite the dream, I still believed I had violated some spiritual code. Inwardly I waited for a heavy load of karma to fall on top of me and crush me. And many things appeared in my path that were obviously paying back the bankruptcy.

They didn't always appear in the arena of money, however. Sometimes it was illness. Or a gift of aid to a friend.

Once the school closed, I had no income. My first challenge was finding a job. But before I could even finish writing my résumé, I got a phone call from a respected doctor in San Francisco.

He had read a review of my low-fat cooking classes. He was working with a university hospital studying heart disease, and he needed someone to run the food program. Would I be interested? He mentioned a salary that practically caused me to drop the phone.

The next door that opened for me was almost more astounding a gift.

I had always wanted to write a cookbook but hadn't found either the time nor the skills to put one together. I couldn't imagine how to go about contacting a publisher or writing a proposal. But during the next month, totally out of the blue, a large West Coast publisher called me.

They had also heard of the school and wondered if I would like to put together one of their cookbooks. The writer they had hired had changed her mind, and they were desperate for someone to take over the work.

Painful Experience, Strong Lesson

By telling this story, I don't want to imply that the ends justify the means.

For me, bankruptcy was a very serious step. It cannot be taken lightly. In most cases, quite a few people are hurt or at least inconvenienced. In this way, it is not a positive option for most of us.

But in the larger picture, I made a decision that was the best possible option for me at the time.

One reason was this: Interwoven in my experience were old attitudes about success and failure that I needed to rid myself of. I needed an important lesson on money too—how to use it wisely and how to budget—things I had never learned. Life taught me a severe lesson with the business I built and lost so quickly.

It's a lesson I don't know if I could've learned another, less painful way.

The severity of such an experience often depends on one thing: How fast can we recognize the experience as one of positive growth and change? And how fast can we see the lesson behind it?

A speaker I once heard gave a good analogy of this: He said that life continually hands him bricks and mortar. If they are left lying around and not used, they will harden into obstacles. And whether he builds a wall or a walkway with the raw material is entirely up to him.

In other words, our approach determines our experience. The Holy Spirit, the essence of life, is very committed to each of us and our spiritual development. Hard lessons and difficult turning points can bring us the strength we will need later. In my story, a painful experience with money gave me a more conservative streak and a new attitude about saving. A very difficult path can prepare you for survival.

But how do you take the leap in understanding and learn to see something beneficial in what appears to be a negative experience?

Borneo Blessing

The Sunday, September 26, 1993, edition of the Minneapolis *Star Tribune* ran an article by a travel photographer who had been on assignment in Borneo when she faced a situation as transforming for her as mine had been for me.

On their way to the Djakarta airport for a flight to a jungle camp in Borneo, she was helping companions load baggage into taxis when she realized she didn't have her camera bag with all her film. She got to the airport in time to see her camera bag, piled with the rest of the group's luggage, go through the security X-ray machine.

X-ray machines in Western countries are film-safe for speeds up to 1000; her film was 1600, and this was a developing country. Sick, she turned from the group to contemplate her loss. Now she had no film for the story she was supposed to shoot in Borneo. Deep in the jungle there were not likely to be camera shops.

After being flown halfway across the world, how would she complete her assignment?

Friends tried to comfort her, but during the plane ride to a small village, she fell deeper and deeper into her greatest fear as a professional photographer: coming home with nothing.

To calm herself she turned to a book of meditations a friend had given her before she left. One sentence jumped out at her: *You can choose how to feel.* She had never believed that. But now she tried. Repeating phrases from the book over and over to herself, she tried to flood out the worry with uplifting words.

And to her surprise, it began to work.

"Without the usual self-torture," she wrote, "I had room for other thoughts—not how awful the past event was, but what to do next."

A friend leading the trip counseled her to not give up. "Why don't you shoot some of the film and get it developed—find out if it really is wrecked?" she suggested. Surprisingly, even though they were now in the deep jungle, there was a photo lab downstream in the last village.

The woman quickly shot a few rolls of the film, handed the boatman the equivalent of twenty dollars, and watched him slip down the river. She crossed her fingers and kept practicing her new vision: You can choose how to feel.

It took two days for the boatman to return, but when he did he was carrying a package of prints. The film had come through unscathed.

To the travel photographer, it was nothing short of miraculous. Which was the greater surprise, she wondered later, finding out that there was a working Fuji photo lab in the jungles of Borneo or learning that she could choose how to feel—a miraculous turning point in itself?

Such experiences as my bankruptcy and the photographer's film disaster are ways the Holy Spirit softens us. Life, through pain and heartache, through giving up a long-held belief or dream that we really want to keep, teaches Soul how to be a greater vehicle for love.

And sometimes it's with the help of another Soul who comes into your life at just the right moment.

In the next chapter, we'll explore how people who come into your life are often spiritual teachers in one sense or another—teachers who can help you travel through difficult turning points with more ease and grace.

9. People Who Teach You

A friend told me an interesting anecdote about a famous statesman. It seems a young assistant to the statesman was asked to research a project and prepare a report. After several weeks of work the young man finally came to the statesman and placed a large folder on his desk. The statesman thanked him, and the young man went away.

The next day, the statesman called the young man into his office.

"Is this the very best you can do?" he asked, pointing to the report.

"Well," said the young man, "maybe I could research it a little more."

"Please do that," said the statesman, handing back the folder.

Two weeks later the young man returned. Again the statesman kept the report overnight and in the morning called the young man into his office.

"Is this the very best you can do?" he asked again. The young man hemmed and hawed, then finally agreed to work on the report a bit more. The statesman again handed it to him, and the young man walked out.

Several days later the young man was back. The process was repeated and again the statesman kept the report overnight and then asked, "Is this the very best you can do?"

"Yes, it is!" the young man exploded. "I have slaved over that report, researched everything I could think of, and rewritten it four times. It's the very best I can do."

"Very well," said the statesman, "I'll read it now."

Carrying Through

We all have people in our lives who teach us these kinds of pointed lessons, lessons which can be turning points in our spiritual growth. I've written several times about my grandmother who taught me so much when I was a child.

One of my grandmother's favorite slogans was "carry through." Her grandchildren were taught exactly what this meant. When you spilled something, you cleaned it up. When you finished playing, you put your toys away. When you said you were going to be someplace, you were there, and on time.

My grandmother valued dependability above everything. And I was the grandchild who exemplified it for her. I grew up with these qualities she so loved engraved on my heart: accountability, being on time, orderliness, and organization.

Until another teacher came along who showed me the missing piece needed to balance my grandmother's teachings.

Our Unexpected Teachers

In my late thirties I became friends with a woman I'll call Rebecca. We were drawn to each other, pulled almost across the room at a meeting. We both ended up working in the same office.

Our working relationship got stronger, and slowly the out-of-work friendship did too. But snags kept arising.

I would expect something from her, based on something she had said or a promise made, and she would not carry through. The biggest disappointment was when we agreed we would meet regularly to work on writing projects, but she fell in love about that time and the meetings dwindled to nothing.

Anger at these disappointments grew in me slowly and became like a knot in my chest. I kept my contact with her to a minimum until eventually we were barely speaking, only making connections in our work.

Why had I trusted her when I knew she was so changeable? But I found I could not just let our relationship die, even if it was hurting me.

One evening after Rebecca failed to show up for yet another writing meeting with me, I began to write about the situation, how it angered and frustrated me, how I felt so cast aside and dishonored by her lack of carrying through. I wrote her name in the center of a piece of paper, then did the turning-point exercise in chapter 8 with any words or phrases that came to mind.

An Old Pattern

As I did the exercise, the intensity of my feelings surprised me.

I felt completely and utterly betrayed by something as small as a missed appointment. I knew that Rebecca was in my life to teach me something, however painful it might be. But for the life of me, I couldn't figure it out.

Sitting in the living room that night, I thought hard about this relationship. At first I was sure I knew what the problem was: Rebecca's attitude about accountability. If she would only do what she said she was going to do, our friendship would be all roses. But then I wondered, *If I took to heart my premise that everyone in my life was here to teach me, what might I learn from Rebecca?*

Was there a more significant aspect to our relationship that I was overlooking?

I worked my way around the page, surprised to find images of my grandmother surfacing, along with notes of her disappointments in life. So many people had disappointed my grandmother—why was that? Were her goals of carrying through and accountability not worthy ones? There was a puzzle to solve here, a link between what I had learned from my grandmother and what I was learning from Rebecca.

Interested in solving the right problem and really understanding the turning point, I began listing the positive traits of our friendship, what I felt I gained from knowing this woman.

Flexibility was one. She found it easy to change, which was a virtue in most cases. In fact, the thing that had attracted me to Rebecca in the beginning was her fluidity, creativity, and easygoing nature. *She also found it easy to forgive,* I thought somewhat shamefaced, as I suddenly recalled all the times I had canceled dates with her.

It took time, but finally the real problem emerged.

I realized that along with many virtues a pattern of rigidity had been passed down from my grandmother to me. Yes, the values my grandmother held dear were worthwhile ones, but along with them came a lack of flexibility. I remembered how hard it was for my grandmother to forgive someone who had wronged her, however slight the mistake. My attraction to this friendship with Rebecca made sense now. I was inwardly pulled toward those people who could balance out the beginnings of intolerance in my nature.

What Am I Learning Here?

Sometimes when I meet someone, I have a certain feeling about them: *This one will be an important teacher for me.*

The feeling is not always altogether pleasant, because there is also the foreknowledge of a turning point and possibly some hard lessons to come. The process of living grinds away our rough edges and many of the people we meet act as sandpaper to further smooth those edges. Somehow this person or that person would be the sandpaper to my rough edges.

One such trait of mine that took some sanding in my twenties and thirties was the need to rearrange my outer life when I became uncomfortable with a slow cycle. In the worst of times, when my job, marriage, or a friendship seemed to bog down, I might rearrange the furniture in the entire house before my roommate got home from work. I remember the face of one such partner, arriving home early one evening and doing a double take as he caught a glimpse of the totally different living room.

I even recall him checking the number outside to make sure he had the right house.

In those days, I moved around easily. I would up and quit a job, end a relationship, move out of the area whenever things got uncomfortable. My slogan seemed to be, If change is coming, I'm going to beat it to the punch. And usually I beat it by many months. In other words, I didn't work with the pace of life, I pushed the envelope. I rushed scenes, I pushed climaxes, and I often spoiled the final act of the play.

Some people have no trouble with this, but it was slowly making me very unhappy. I didn't realize that I was living on an edge of impatience, that I was changing for change's sake, moving furniture and partners to avoid working with the natural flow of life. It wasn't until my midthirties that I began to get an inkling of what truly happy people understand with their whole being: that life has a natural order and flow.

Change happens within when it is right in the larger sense.

It was not long after this concept found its way into my heart that I met my husband. The first time we dated was a paradox of uneasy and rapturous feelings. The uneasiness was born of a brief moment when I felt like I was drowning. I knew I was over my head with him from the start; he would teach me plenty.

In a typically rushed move, I quit my job, found another one in the city where he lived, and hired a moving van to pack with my furniture.

I remember the day the van arrived, the movers unloading box after box into the garage and roomfuls of furniture into his once-spacious, one-bedroom apartment. Immediately I set about arranging everything, like a demon whipping through the apartment as my future husband looked on. Finally he stopped me.

"Let's do this together, think a little about where things should go," he said.

Here was a new concept: planning from the inside out, not the way I had always done it.

Over and over in the first three years we were together, he gently but firmly showed me how much easier life could be when one listened to and followed life's natural rhythm. Each time I wanted to rush my fences, he presented a different option—usually waiting.

As if setting sail in a small boat, I could wait for the wind to fill my sails and allow me to glide away from the mooring. I had always been rowing out, never waiting for the wind.

Meeting Life's Teachers

Often the best teachers in my life have been the hardest ones.

When I was a high-school student I had a teacher named Claire. Claire taught Russian and history in the small Quaker school I attended in Baltimore. A strict and exacting teacher, she was my own personal cross to bear for four long years. Yet she taught me more about self-discipline in those four years than any other teacher I have ever had.

I had begun studying Russian before my family moved from New York, mostly through the influence of my best friend, Masha. Masha's family was from Russia. She had long blond hair, a silvery laugh, and a manner that spoke "Russian princess" to me. I wanted to be like her.

So I signed up for Russian classes when I was in seventh grade.

The first step to becoming a Russian princess—learning the language—was incredibly difficult for me, and I am still amazed at how I persevered.

I had no particular talent for the language, just a burning desire to be able to converse with Masha and her family when I went there for dinner. I did have a strong feeling for Russia and the Russian culture, an affinity I couldn't explain.

The next year my father was transferred from New York to Maryland, and my teary good-bye to Masha and her family was punctuated by excitement over living in a new city and making new friends. The new school had an even stronger language program, and I signed up for both Russian and French. I dreamed of writing Masha letters in Russian someday.

Those next four years were grueling, to say the least. Claire was renowned nationwide for her teaching expertise and her toughness.

I drilled verbs, vocabulary, idioms, and pronunciation until I dreamed in Russian, but it still didn't come easy. Claire wanted to turn me from a casual student into one who excelled, and the missing ingredient was self-discipline. She made sure I developed plenty in those four years.

I graduated and was grateful to finally be rid of Claire's assignments, but it wasn't more than six years later that I saw her again.

Strangely enough, it was through the vitamin business that I had for three years. Claire was given some of the vitamins by a friend but hadn't known where she could buy more. The company gave her my address.

Meeting Claire again as an adult was an entirely new experience. She still had the same exacting manner but beneath it I could now see a warm heart and a deep love for teaching. We began corresponding each time I sent her a box of vitamins. Soon our letters took on a spiritual tone, as she began to tell me of her studies in Theosophy.

I had just become a member of ECKANKAR and sent her a book, which she read.

Questions started. Although Theosophy remained her primary spiritual interest, Claire was always curious about ECKANKAR, and we shared many deep discussions about Soul, reincarnation, and spiritual masters.

Looking back on this unusual friendship, I realize that as the circle was completed I was able to share something of myself with my mentor, just as she had when she taught me self-discipline via the Russian language. Like my grandmother, Claire was a believer in the higher disciplines of life, like doing your best and carrying through. And in those years of language classes and our spiritual discussions, some of this rubbed off on me.

Above Karma

We may meet people because of ties from the past, debts to be resolved, or love to exchange. This is the pull of karma.

But we also meet people because we have something to teach and something to learn. I found keeping this viewpoint puts me in the higher consciousness of Soul, rather than in the push and pull of karma. Viewing each relationship as a spiritual opportunity to learn about myself helps me become more aware of the next lesson I have coming.

Often, a trait I see in the other person will be exactly what I need to learn about. Or maybe I need to review some spiritual law or life skill that this person has mastered.

Animal Teachers

During the experience with my friend Rebecca, I was suffering from too little of a quality that is common to people who face turning points easily. This quality is spontaneity. Spontaneous people are often more alert to turning points, willing to let go of what they have to get something better.

To foster spontaneity, life brought me a teacher in the form of a small dog named BJ.

My husband first broached the idea of getting a miniature long-haired dachshund puppy. Being a cat person, I had never spent much time around dogs and was both excited and hesitant. Wouldn't a dog cover my clean white sofa with muddy paw prints, wake me up in the middle of the night to go out, and generally disturb my carefully wrought patterns of living?

BJ did all this and more. He turned my life upside down for three months of his first winter with us.

And despite my irritation and despair over the sofa and my lack of sleep, I knew this little dog was to be an important teacher for me. The main lesson he teaches me every day is how to be full of joy and spontaneity.

BJ teaches by example. Whenever we meet, he greets me like a long-lost friend. No matter how his

day has gone, he always expects the best from me —
a pat on the head, a session of catch with one of his
tennis balls, his dinner.

There is no doubt in his mind that I love him and
I will give him the best I have.

Expanding Vision

BJ's arrival changed other members of our house-
hold as well. Our two cats, Sasha and Sushi, had
settled into a comfortable hierarchy, with Sushi
definitely being top cat.

When she first saw the tiny puppy, she knew her
life had changed—and she decided it was for the
worse. Irritated that we had brought this stranger
to live with us, Sushi retired to the basement and
backyard for three months.

Sasha took a different tack. He became the kindly
uncle to BJ.

It was amazing to watch the thin, eight-year-old
cat escorting the young puppy around the house.
Sasha even tolerated BJ's playful rolling and tum-
bling, tennis-ball-chasing, and mild biting. The cat
made it his job to show BJ the spots for afternoon
sunning, the windows with the best view of passersby, and the most comfortable cushion for morning
naps.

Before BJ, Sasha had been extremely fearful. He
was always startled when someone came in the room;
if I dropped a book on the floor, he would dash
downstairs. The sound of the vacuum cleaner or
other noises terrified him.

Maybe it was because Sasha felt responsible for
BJ, but the puppy's noises never startled the cat.

And this new bravery leaked over into the rest of Sasha's life.

Now he sits placidly when we vacuum, not even moving a whisker.

Sushi finally came out of the basement one weekend. She too had changed. Having ruled the roost for eight years, she had grown used to ignoring the people in her life except for basic needs, such as food and water. Now she was less sure of her position in the hierarchy.

She realized she needed more than food and water: she needed love.

Moving quickly from haughty to ingratiating, she began spending mornings in the kitchen, waiting for us to wake up so she could tell us the happenings of the night in her loud Siamese voice. BJ had opened her eyes to what she could contribute to the family as well as receive.

People—and other beings—who handle change well rarely have tunnel vision about themselves or their life. They are able to step above a situation and put it in a larger framework.

In the next chapter we'll explore how this quality helps you face major life changes, such as birth, death, marriage, and divorce.

10. Major Changes, Major Blessings

The turning points we've talked about have ranged from dramatic to subtle, but none have been life-or-death experiences. Yet every day people face the possibility of death through disease, war, accident, or other disaster.

Many crumble. Yet many come through the experience with renewed strength—and faith that a divine hand was guiding them even in the darkest moments.

What quality of character makes the difference here? An attitude of seeing the blessings within each experience life offers.

Lesson in a Car Accident

In the 1986 *ECK Mata Journal,* a yearly magazine of stories by members of ECKANKAR, an ECKist wrote of a car accident that turned her life upside down.

The morning of the accident she had woken with a sense of joy, as if great blessings were about to enter her life. That evening, she put her two-year-old daughter into the front seat of their car, snug amongst a huge bag of laundry, then drove off for home.

On the way, they were hit head-on by a truck. Miraculously, Ann's daughter Sarah remained unhurt, protected by the laundry bag. Ann, however, had not gotten off easily. She was rushed to the hospital where doctors gingerly extracted slivers of glass from her tongue and stitched the cuts on her head. Singing HU, she was able to calm herself and made it through the emergency. In time she was on her way to full recovery.

When she got home, she saw a letter she had written the morning of the accident, thanking Sri Harold Klemp for the blessings about to come into her life. *How was a near-fatal car accident a blessing?* she wondered. The answer came in the next few months.

Recovery gave Ann plenty of mental and emotional rest and Sarah special time with her father. The situation was indeed a blessing.

It only took a different viewpoint for Ann to see past the trauma of the accident to the gift, a gift she might not have been able to receive another way.

Crisis Living

An ECK teacher once led a workshop where she asked participants to graph the highs and lows of turning points in their lives, including supposedly disastrous ones such as accidents, divorces, marriages, job shifts.

The graphs showed an interesting pattern.

Participants marked the crises as low spots on the graphs, and the teacher noticed that the lower the dip, the higher the upswing that followed. Each major upheaval in the form of disaster, disease, or disability was followed by turned fortunes and new understandings. Divine Spirit is very efficient in the way It works.

In my life, crisis appears to be particularly needed in two situations: (1) when I need a good shaking up spiritually, when old patterns that no longer serve me have gotten too deeply rooted and need to be weeded out. Or (2) when a large amount of karma, or past debt, presents itself to be worked off, as in the following story.

My Summer of Cancer

In the summer of 1988 I discovered I had cancer. Although it was a truly frightening experience, many blessings came to me and my family through this dramatic turning point.

It all began with a routine blood test. I had been feeling tired, and at my checkup I asked the doctor to run a thyroid panel. The numbers showed possible malfunction of the thyroid. On the advice of the doctor, I made an appointment with an endocrinologist.

The specialist dismissed the blood-test numbers but was immediately curious about my thyroid, which protruded slightly on the right side of my neck.

"What's this lump on your neck?" he asked.

"Oh, it's been there for years. Probably a result of a car accident; the muscle's strained."

"Not a muscle strain," he said. "I'll be right back."

He stepped out of the room and returned with a lab technician. "This might be a tumor," he said. "We can perform a biopsy right now and see what the tissue looks like."

Later that week, I called the clinic for the results. "The tissue shows abnormal patterns. It could be cancer," my doctor said. "We'd like to do a radioactive scan on the tumor. Can you come in next week?"

My mind was awhirl. I was seeing my life change before my eyes: disease, death—my worst fears were being realized. *Cancer,* I thought. *Oh, my God.*

Help Is Always There

I closed my eyes and desperately asked for help and guidance.

The reassurance came from the Mahanta, my inner guide, "I'll be there. Go ahead with it." I asked the doctor for some time to think this over. His parting admonition was not to take too much time. The scan later that week showed a good possibility of a malignancy, and an operation was advised.

The Holy Spirit was beginning to stir depths of myself that I had been afraid to examine for centuries. I shook inside for days, as one dire possibility after another surfaced.

My mother suggested flying to Baltimore, Maryland; the family knew doctors at Johns Hopkins Hospital. We would find the best surgeon, the best oncologist. The telephone wires hummed between Baltimore and Minneapolis almost every night, as my family rallied to my support. The event was causing a vast healing on all levels: we were closer to each other than we had been in years.

The day of the surgery I was in a daze. Feeling the Inner Master quite close, but palms sweaty with fear and an even bigger lump in my throat, I was wheeled into the operating room. I joked halfheartedly with the anesthesiologist that I would be his best patient.

That was the last thing I remembered.

Remembering My True Mission

I found myself in a beautiful city in another world. All my dreams had come true. I had somehow escaped all fear, pain, and death. A young Adonis romanced me.

He said he loved me and wanted me to stay forever in the lovely place he had created. In return he promised to take away all the fears that had clouded my life on earth. The inner world was huge, light, and happy; people lived by creating music and art instead of working. It seemed as though I had everything, but a thought kept intruding: *Where was my Inner Master?*

The young man showed me the place where I would live. I was entranced by the spaciousness, the lovely feeling.

At one point I put my hand in my pocket and was surprised to find a folded slip of paper. I knew the Master had written two words on it. They were two things I loved very much in my life on earth. Not easy things, but things that were helping me work out my fears and grow stronger. Although it was the more difficult road, I knew that in my earthly life I was experiencing great tempering as Soul.

It was tempting to stay in this place of beauty and light, where I knew no fear, but I had to return to earth to complete the work I had begun. This was my choice. Reluctantly I told the young man I had to go back.

He protested and tried to keep me; I realized later this was my struggle to reenter the physical body.

Unexpected Gifts

Although only hours had passed, it seemed like days. I was floating above my body as it lay in the recovery room. I knew I had to go back, although it took all the effort I could muster to move my hand and slowly come back to consciousness.

Later my mother told me it had taken hours to revive me in the recovery room. I had been so pale and deathlike.

She never knew how close to the truth that was. All that night I struggled with the choice I had made. The world where my fears had miraculously dissolved seemed even more appealing now. Dying seemed a positive choice when my body was so full of pain. Everything hurt, and I was nauseous from the anesthesia. My throat felt empty, as if more than a cancerous tumor had been removed.

The loneliness of returning to this gray world was overwhelming.

But the Inner Master had been there all along — not visible, but in those two written words. I later came to understand that the place I had visited while my body lay unconscious was in the lower heavens; the young man had tried to trick me into settling for less than my destiny. My sense of obligation to return, to work out my fears, had saved me from a beautiful trap.

It was not until months later that I began to piece together the puzzle of this important turning point.

It felt like a weight had been removed from me and also that I had passed a test of courage. Now I have gained a chance to reach a much higher heaven than that which the beautiful young man had offered me.

Part of my decision not to die was a feeling of responsibility to pay back debts I'd incurred and finish learning the lessons that accompanied them. During the months following my cancer operation and treatment, I was able to let go of very deep-seated fears about myself, as well as reunite with my family. I also felt that I had somehow paid back some old karma I had incurred during the years I had had the cooking school. Spirit chose this very efficient way to handle both in one short life-and-death experience.

The insights and healings that followed my summer of cancer were indeed highs on my graph for that year.

Getting through the Tunnel

When I was young, my mother would drive us kids each July from Baltimore to upstate New York where we attended my grandmother's summer camp. On one part of the New York State Thruway, we had to drive through a long tunnel. Mom hated tunnels. So she sang her way through them.

Perhaps she was afraid of getting stuck in the darkness and never being able to find her way out. Through my cancer experience, I understood that feeling.

Sometimes it was as if I were singing in the darkness, trying to get through the tunnel of the experience. But since I was given the blessing of my experience with cancer and made a conscious decision to stay and finish my work, I no longer view life as a tunnel to be sung through.

Instead, my life has become one of simple steps from one experience to the next.

This understanding wasn't instantaneous or neatly packaged. It came to me very slowly, through months of recording my dreams and daily experiences. It came because I wanted to know.

Death of a Loved One

A dear friend had to face death at an important crossroads in her life—the death of her beloved husband of many years. Normally this would be devastating, and this is not to say that it was easy for her. But because she was paying attention, life prepared her in an unexpected way for this major turning point. Her story was in the 1994 *ECKANKAR Journal.*

One Saturday morning, my friend was on her way to the post office when she took a wrong turn. Instead of turning left, she turned right and had to double back through a series of unfamiliar roads.

As soon as she turned down the unfamiliar route, she felt a holy silence everywhere. She rounded a curve and saw a man in the middle of the road. Her first thought was, *He's a runner who's had a heart attack.* She parked the car on the side of the road and got out to see if she could help.

When she stepped out of the car, she saw his terrible wounds and knew he'd been hit by a car and there wasn't much time.

She looked at him. "I'll be right back," she said. "May the blessings be." This is an ancient blessing in ECKANKAR. It helps release the outcome of the event, however traumatic, into the hands of Divine Spirit.

She ran to the nearest house, yelling, "Call 911! Call for help!" They did. Then she ran back to the man and knelt beside him, singing HU, an ancient name for God.

The first few notes came out as sobs. My friend heard the Inner Master chide her, "You have a task to do. Focus on it." So she centered herself, and the HU came out as clear as a bell.

The man's body suddenly stopped spasming. He turned and looked my friend in the eye. She knew Soul was recognizing the Light and Sound of God in the HU she sang. Suddenly my friend's inner hearing opened, and she could hear the man speaking. His only concern was for his family. "My wife, my family," he said silently, "please let them know."

She said aloud to God, "How can I do this? This man doesn't have any identification on him."

The next minute, another man stopped his car and ran over. "Can I help?" he asked. Then, as he knelt down beside my friend, he gasped, "Oh, my God, it's Stan."

"Do you know this man?" she asked.

He nodded yes.

"Please, go get his family. He wants his family to know."

The man turned to obey, and the injured man relaxed as soon as he knew this was taken care of. His next concern was voiced to her silently: "I need the blessings of God."

My friend felt strength surge into her heart. In a clear voice she said, "You have earned the right to walk in the presence of God. You have learned love and compassion, and giving of yourself in this lifetime. You will forever live in the worlds of God."

Soon the paramedics came and put the man in an ambulance. My friend continued to kneel on the side of the road, silently singing HU. A few minutes later, a branch fell from a tree and landed gently beside her. She knew this Soul had translated from this world in the process we call death.

My friend's life was changed by witnessing the passing of another person in such a dramatic way. A few short weeks later, her own husband died. His death was not unexpected since he had been in and out of hospitals for kidney failure for many years. But their love for each other was a strong bond, and his leaving shocked her to the core.

Witness to Great Change

One day, not long after her husband's funeral, my friend received a letter from the wife of the man who had died on the side of the road.

In the letter, the wife explained she had read an announcement about my friend's husband in the paper. She wanted to express her sympathy and also tell my friend how much it had meant to her to have the ECKist's support when her own husband, Stan, had passed away.

The two women shared a common experience. For both, losing a beloved spouse was life-changing, shocking, and the last thing they had wished for.

But it was not life-destroying.

Because of the belief that their spouses had in some way chosen to make this step, each woman saw a spiritual side of the experience of death, believing that Soul continues to live on.

Death makes us feel very vulnerable. It reminds us that despite our best efforts at controlling life, there are certain things beyond our control. Yet both myself and the two women in the story above have learned that Soul, the essence of a person, does have a choice when death comes.

Death is only another turning point, a door to the next room. We can choose how we view the process of death.

There's an ancient Hindu proverb that says that if a fish swims up the mountain stream, it will be bruised against the rocks, exhaust itself, and dislike the journey. If the fish swims with the current, however, it easily avoids the rocks, travels swiftly, and enjoys the journey. The stream doesn't care which way the fish swims.

Life is the stream that pulls us along on an inevitable course that leads to the death of the physical body. There are ways to delay death but no way to outsmart it.

And why would we want to? What we have here is not anywhere near as wonderful as what we have in the higher worlds. The goal is not to avoid death but to make our swim in the stream of life easier, by going with the current.

One way to do this is to live life fully but prepare for the ultimate spiritual turning point that awaits us.

This is not to condone a morbid fascination with death and dying. Life is for living fully; that's why we're here. But if the fear of death is strong within you, it hampers your ability to live fully. The best way I know to prepare for the process of death is to learn conscious awareness of the heavens that lie beyond this world.

Through dreams, we can be taken to these heavens and even come to know our home in the next life.

⁙ Exercise: Visiting the Heavens of God

An exercise you can practice to become aware of the inner worlds is this: Each night before sleep, ask either the Mahanta, the Living ECK Master or another spiritual figure you trust, "Please take me on an inner journey to the heavens of God. Take me to that place which will benefit me spiritually."

Make careful notes of any and all dream experiences you remember.

This exercise will bring results, but they may be subtle, like incomprehensible pieces of a puzzle. You may not get any clue about the inner heavens until you have noted the images or feelings from several weeks or months of nighttime journeys.

In the next chapter, we'll look at how knowledge of past lives can help us with present turning points.

11. Past Lives and Present Turning Points

Not everyone is fortunate enough to have pristine recall of past lives. Mine come in dribs and drabs. Often I'll have a strong feeling for a place or person—without a clue as to why. In the past five years, three strong incidents have come to the fore, all past-life experiences that influenced the present.

A turning point for me was realizing just how these lives were affecting me today, in subtle—and not so subtle—ways.

I faced them at first without many skills or tools. These turning points weren't great outer changes; they were inner realizations. They required me to take less outer and more inner action. By the time the third incident emerged, I had begun to suspect just how the past was affecting the present.

I was better prepared to read the signs.

The first story involves what was planned to be a pleasant camping trip my husband and I took one summer after we had moved to Minnesota. The second started in Paris, France, on a short journey one summer with my younger sister. The third is about repeated visits to the Black Hills of South Dakota and what I discovered there.

Parent Lake

Several summers ago my husband and I started packing for our first canoe trip. I had always been uneasy about being alone in the wilderness, even though it pulls me with its intense beauty. My childhood summers were spent canoeing lakes in the Adirondacks of upstate New York near my grandmother's summer camp. Now living only a six-hour drive from the remote Boundary Waters wilderness area of northern Minnesota, I imagined, with pleasure, paddling remote lakes under cloudless skies.

As we packed I was blissfully unaware of how my underlying unease had gotten hold of the planning, but it began to show in the heaps of food I wanted to bring.

Nothing seemed enough. Every trip to the store brought home one more freeze-dried package, another bag of fruit or candy bars, a couple more boxes of emergency rations.

The pile grew in a corner of the living room—more than a week's worth of rations for a family of five.

Driving north that weekend was a gentle process of shedding the familiar cities. We passed patchwork fields and neat farmlands, going deeper into the unknown territory of the wilderness. We stopped to visit farm stands and a roadside restaurant.

The day was warm and pleasant, and the bright blue canoe shone on the roof rack in the sunlight.

As we neared the wilderness area that afternoon, I grew drowsy and lethargic, lulled by the gentle sounds of the car. In my half-sleep, the scent of the pine woods filled the air and a strange dream crossed my vision.

* * *

I stood in a sunlit forest clearing, dressed in greasy buckskin, the tight loop of beaded band on my forearm. I knew I was alone, and it frightened me very much. A tight band also gripped my heart; for some reason I knew I must be very quiet. The name Monegwa came to mind.

* * *

The car jolted, and I woke suddenly, a cold, constricted feeling in my chest.

I didn't mention the experience to my husband, not wanting to disturb his long-awaited vacation. But inner information was coming fast, in vivid inner visions, and I wondered what I had naïvely set in motion with this trip.

We arrived at Snowbank, the first lake, toward evening. Our plan was to paddle across the lake and spend the night at a shoreside campsite, then portage the canoe to a second, more remote lake the next morning. But I convinced my husband to push on, in the few hours of light left in the summer evening.

I made it sound easy: a relaxed paddle to the portage trail, maybe a mile to carry our gear and canoe, then another lake to cross as the sun set behind the trees.

The remote lake is Parent, isolated and accessible only by air, paddle, or foot.

As we loaded the canoe, I joked about the abundant food supplies, then silently added more packages to the space beneath my canoe seat, not sure why it was so important but wishing I'd brought even more. We set off across Snowbank, enjoying the slanting rays of evening light and the sound of other

133

canoeists in the distance. When we reached the portage trail on the far side, we discovered the canoe was too heavy with supplies to lift out of the water, so we unloaded it and began carrying the first of many boxes and bags up the root-strewn dirt trail that led to Parent Lake.

My first glimpse of Parent Lake gave me an unexplained shock. It looked eerie in the setting sun, a bank of dark clouds casting an almost greenish light over the surface.

Much rougher than Snowbank, the water was thrashed by a sharp wind that caused waves to lap aggressively against the rocky shoreline. Our paddles pushing through the water like heavy spoons in a vat of molasses, we slowly worked our way across the rough lake. The shoreline, studded with deformed pines and ravaged by the wind, hung dark shadows over the lake's surface in the twilight.

It seemed to take forever to reach our campsite, and as we pulled the canoe onto a rocky beach, I was again overcome by an almost incapacitating drowsiness and great sadness.

What was going on?

The uncomfortable feelings paralyzed me until I was unable to perform the simplest task, even unpacking a pot to boil water for tea. The sun was setting rapidly now, and I sat hunched on a fallen log while my husband set up the tent and started the cooking fire. The feeling that overcame me, shutting out all others, was that I would die soon, in this place, and no one would know.

The stupor continued through the evening. That night, before I fell into a light sleep, I listened for a long time to a pair of loons calling and laughing across the lake.

The comforting sound counteracted the deep sadness I felt and relaxed my heart. I seemed to remember someone I loved telling me a story about loons—God's gentlest birds—protecting the frail beings in this world. I drifted to sleep listening to their almost-human cries and smelling the strong piney scent of the trees that encircled the clearing.

* * *

In my dream I am again Monegwa, and I am sitting on a fallen log, stiff with misery. I have walked all day to this remote clearing on the shore of a small lake. I am very far from my home territory, which is good because my parents want to kill me. I have observed them commit a heinous crime against the tribe. They have lied to the elders, and I am blamed. My grandmother has secreted me out of the camp at night, taking me to a trail that stretched in the distance.

Seven years old, hardly a man, I must go into the wilderness alone and try to survive.

Sitting in the clearing surrounded by pines, I remember my grandmother's parting words. She has told me to listen for the loon, the bird of laughter and joy, my protector in this life. The loon, she says, will remind me that there are those in the tribe who still love me. Leaving her I feel great sadness, and fear pulls at my heart. The harsh beauty of the wilderness offers me little comfort.

Because I am weak with sadness and unable to stir myself to find food or make a fire, I die in the clearing a few days later.

* * *

The dream was only a faint memory as we packed up early the next morning and paddled away from the pine clearing on the shore of Parent Lake. The farther we went, the better I felt. Our canoe glided swiftly over the now-glassy water, and the portage trail was sunlit and mostly downhill. The first thing I heard when we arrived back at Snowbank was the clear, happy sounds of children's laughter echoing from a nearby cove.

The window that opened at Parent Lake on Monegwa's life and death dramatically brought to the fore my unease with being alone in the wilderness. But it didn't fully erase it, because at first I had almost no memory of the two visions and the dream. Pieces to the puzzle of what had happened that night came to my awareness very slowly over the next few months.

Because I wanted to solve the mystery of that lifetime and ease the strong feelings of fear in this one, I paid close attention to the road map the Mahanta, the Inner Master, gave me to uncover the memories I had buried.

Slowly I was able to see that I needed to resolve a past life that was still affecting the present one. That resolution was a major turning point for me.

Feelings like these are often clues. They intrude into the present when it is time for Soul to face something from the past, reconcile or understand it, and move on. I had a chance to gain a broader perspective, but the information I received about my life as an Indian boy came in fits and starts.

Eventually there was a healing, and I made peace with that life.

It was the process of writing these feelings and images that allowed me to see this wilderness experience as a spiritual turning point. It was a big release of past karma, allowing me to forgive myself and others in that life. It moved me into a new level of trust that life could and would take care of me, as Soul—as it hadn't taken care of a small Indian boy alone on the shores of Parent Lake.

Past to Present—Both Turning Points

Reliving this experience was not easy. Since then, I've not been very comfortable with the wilderness, although I love its beauty and long to spend time there. I've tried, but even traveling down the road toward the Boundary Waters wilderness area causes cold sweats and great angst. If I stay to the lakeshore of Superior, out of the pine trees and away from the deep forests, I am fine.

That lifetime involved turning points about trust and about truth.

I had told what I knew as the truth, was cast out, and died horribly. In this life, I have been very outspoken but it has always been tempered with a sense of reserve.

I know that truth is more relative, less black and white, than I knew it as a young Indian boy.

The turning point came about when I visited Parent Lake and experienced the fear and sadness of Monegwa's life. But most important was my spiritual assignment: to figure out a lesson of that life, the telling of truth, and begin to understand where it fit in the present.

Discovering the Story

One Saturday afternoon, my husband and I were having a late lunch at a natural foods restaurant in Minneapolis. I was feeling balanced and good, usually the state of mind I have to have to get clear on a past-life puzzle, so I began talking about how strange our camping trip to Parent Lake had been. I told him about the extremely strong emotions I still felt were associated with the place, a clue that there was something worth looking at, something I was not remembering.

He suggested I begin jotting down images and feelings I remembered from the trip.

I had a small notebook in my purse. So I took it out and wrote down several phrases that came to mind: "blue sky," "bright blue canoe on car roof," "gray waters of Parent Lake, waves crashing, feeling so tired and lonesome, hopeless," "sounds of children calling across Snowbank Lake when we turned back for home." I didn't have much of a clue as to how these images would add up as I was writing. But because I had agreed with Divine Spirit to see what the experience had held for me, I began learning more.

That week memory of the dreams and vision about Monegwa came. I didn't recall his name right away; one morning I had an image in contemplation of an Indian boy, and I silently wondered what his name was. It popped into my head.

I tried a writing exercise. I began creating a "fictional" story based on a camping trip and past-life recall. Like an unfolding dream, the pieces came. I knew they were not fiction; they were mine. I collected parts in my journal from dreams, a passing remark I overheard, a sentence I read in a book.

138

And so I discovered my own story.

Like items in a treasure hunt, the clues to past lives are often hidden in unexpected places. I had to want to find them. I have a good imagination, and that made it easier for me to accept the stray images that floated in. The story rarely unfolded in logical sequence, so I had to be patient, then unscramble what I received.

Cathar Lifetime

The next story connected with the lesson of Monegwa's lifetime in a very neat and efficient way. It also became a turning point about speaking the truth, but in a different way.

I became an ECKist, a member of ECKANKAR, in 1975, twenty years ago. It wasn't until 1993 that I began to realize I had a deep fear of telling others about ECKANKAR. I believed wholeheartedly in individual freedom to choose a spiritual path, so I tried not to push my beliefs on another.

But my reluctance went beyond that.

I was actually afraid of talking to people who asked me, even begged me, for information. So Divine Spirit decided to give me a window into the past to look through and let go of this fear.

It arranged for me to go to Paris one July for the annual ECK European Seminar. Unexpectedly, a month before I left, my younger sister called from Baltimore. She had had a brilliant idea: Since she was due a vacation away from kids and husband, could she join me in Paris for a week of sightseeing?

Ann knew very little about ECK. We didn't have a strong religious background in our family, although we attended a Quaker school until college. But my family prized tradition and intellectual pursuits, and I was afraid of ridicule if I shared ECK with them. I was afraid of the scorn and joking, so rather than risk that I kept ECK largely to myself for almost twenty years.

I knew that if my sister joined me in Paris, it would be inevitable that she would ask about ECKANKAR. I would be meeting her in between seminar activities; there was no way to avoid it. The hotel would be teeming with ECKists too.

The deep-seated fear was beginning to surface, but over it was a love for my sister and a delight in the thought of spending a week vacationing with her.

So I said yes.

Ann was coming from Baltimore, I from Minneapolis, but we were to meet in Boston for the flight to France. Her connecting flight came in after mine, and I waited at the gate, checking my watch to make sure we'd still make the Paris plane. With twenty minutes to spare, we ran for the international terminal, lugging Ann's carry-on baggage. By the time we boarded, most of the passengers were already seated.

As Ann and I, out of breath, made our way down the aisle to our midplane seats, I happened to notice Sri Harold Klemp and his wife, Joan, seated on the right.

Operating from a point much higher than my previous fears about Ann and ECK, I reached down to tap Joan on the shoulder. "I'd like you to meet my sister," I said. Sri Harold cordially shook Ann's hand, and we made small talk for a few seconds before the steward swept us into our seats.

Ann had questions. Who was that man? Was he the head of ECK? And would I please tell her—

finally—exactly what ECK was?

During the week in Paris, Ann had a lot of opportunity to hear about ECK. Everywhere we went, friends from past seminars greeted me and were introduced to her. "Isn't the seminar wonderful?" they'd exclaim, and I'd agree. Ann and I had discussions about my reluctance to share ECK with my family, and I got up the courage to ask her to attend the Sunday session, which she did.

When I got back to the States, I realized I had opened an inner floodgate.

The fear of sharing ECK became more intense for a few months, and yet it seemed everyone was asking. Women in my Saturday group, my cooking assistant at classes, our neighbor down the street—all wanted to know. There was no avoiding it, without seeming rude.

Each time I spoke to someone about ECKANKAR, I found myself reacting very severely afterward. I would literally be in a cold sweat, my stomach in knots, trembling inside.

The past-life connection was made when a friend at work passed on a novel she had finished.

The story took place in ancient France, mostly the Languedoc region in the south. The characters were Cathars, members of a small religious band who broke away from the Catholic church. They were considered heretics but flourished in that area of France for many years before being wiped out by the church and nobles. As many as two hundred were massacred in a single incident, sent to a fiery death.

As I read their story, I felt without a doubt that I had been in the Cathar movement, perhaps not in the massacre but certainly persecuted for my beliefs.

The Cathar beliefs seemed very primitive to me, compared to my present-life understanding of God, but I felt a strong connection with the Cathar people. Without knowing why, I felt they were good people, dedicated to their understanding of God, right and wrong, and a simple desire to live within their beliefs. Because they were seen as a threat to the church in that region of France, they had been exterminated.

Like a disease purged from the body, the fear of talking about my religion has slowly left me.

Now I feel less of a sudden clench in my gut when someone asks me to share ECKANKAR. I now know where the fear came from. I understand that once it was a survival tool for me, and I also know I have reached the turning point in the road where I can let it go.

Exercise: Letting Go of Past Fear

Sri Harold Klemp writes, "When we can fill ourselves with this love of God more and more, finally there is no room in our heart for the darkness of fear." The idea is to get so much love inside that there is no room for fear.

Close your eyes, relax, and ask this simple question inside:

What can I do to get rid of fear and have more love?

Accept whatever comes. Take a minute afterward to write down your answer or image, and reflect on it as you read the last story in this chapter.

Deep Healing

Awareness of past lives only comes when we are ready to receive it.

It's not useful to Soul's journey to have a lot of extra information about the past or future—unless it is helpful to the growth in the present moment. I receive my information only as I can make use of it and grow. Mostly I get glimpses of lifetimes when I was helpful, stood true to my values, or was a heroine who died courageously. Spirit has hidden from me many of the lives when I was on the wrong side of truth, when I did dastardly deeds or hurt others.

This last story is a recent gift from Divine Spirit— which apparently had decided that I could use some less-than-complimentary information about myself in order to wrap up another turning point.

Ever since I moved to Minnesota, I've wanted to spend time in South Dakota and Wyoming. The rugged, arid land draws me strongly. Others remark on its dullness; to me it is beautiful in its subtle colors and harsh landscape. I convinced my husband one summer to take a driving trip for ten days that would include the two states; we would make up our itinerary as we drove.

Everything went fine until we reached Rapid City, South Dakota, the edge of the Black Hills.

We took a motel room there for the night, on the outskirts of town. I remember a thriller being on television and watching until I fell into an uneasy sleep. My dreams were about Native Americans, the 1800s, and scenes right out of the movie *Dances with Wolves*.

I woke in the night with an incredible feeling of

regret—horrible regret. But I had no idea where it came from.

The feeling cleared as we left the Black Hills and did not resurface until we tried another trip the next year. The same thing happened. As soon as we passed the Badlands and saw the forest-covered mountains at the edge of the state, I'd experience it again: deep regret. Once I got hysterical, crying that I'd lost something I could never get back, and that I hadn't meant to do it.

Light didn't dawn on this experience until the fourth summer.

My husband and I were standing at an overlook along one of the highways through the Badlands, when I saw a vision of him falling slowly over the side. It came with an incredible urge to push him over the cliff. I was shocked, disgusted, and afraid at this. We have a loving relationship, and there's no way I'd want to hurt him. But there it was—and with it came the familiar Black-Hills-vacation feeling of deep regret.

"Step back," I cried, my mind filled with images of his body hurtling to the rocks below us.

He looked at me strangely. "Are you all right?"

I could hardly speak, overcome with a sense of protectiveness and aghast at these black feelings within myself. It took days and weeks for the feelings to sort out. I realized that again it was a past life coming up to be accepted, dealt with—this negative side of my character and a black deed I had committed against my brother in a past lifetime as a Native American in the Black Hills.

The turning point from that lifetime was to be able to accept myself as a full person, who had done

144

good things and bad things, who had been the victim and the killer.

Past lives are rarely rosy things. We don't especially need to remember the bright spots; more often it's the darker ones that are the best teachers.

In the final chapter, we'll see how, despite the unexpected challenges of facing turning points, there is always protection as we make our way through them.

12. Protection and the Currents of Change

Through my own and others' stories, I've been trying to illustrate an important principle: turning points are to be embraced rather than avoided.

They are gifts from Divine Spirit, windows we may climb through to the next spiritual level. This is because we are Soul, a creative force in life. To no longer be the victim of change is to see the hand of God at work and to begin creating a life that reflects this understanding.

Most of us manage this every now and then. Maybe you can remember times in your own life when it seemed as if you stood in the calm eye of the hurricane. Events whirled around you, but you felt accepting and at peace.

You felt a certainty that God was in charge.

We can relax in that state. While we know we are the creative force behind our changes, we also know God is in control of the pace of those events. This brings us protection through the currents of change.

Each time I can turn anything—my writing career, my friendships, my living situation, my businesses—

over to God and see the miracles that come to me, I realize how rarely do I actually know what's best for me in the largest sense. I stop trying to manipulate my life based on what I know, from my limited, human perspective. I state my preferences but let God bring me gifts beyond my imagining. It leaves me living in a state of joy.

When I can do this, I also begin to see how carefully I am watched over and protected as I move through my turning points. The following story illustrates the depth of that protection—and God's always-perfect timing.

Chimney Repair

When my husband and I decided to sell our home and move into my dream house, the prospective buyer had to have the property appraised for their loan. An appraiser would come to check the home and verify that the house was worth the loan amount being requested.

One of the ongoing problems we had dealt with during our years in that house was a stucco-covered chimney.

It sat on the south wall of the home, and long cracks ran across it. Each summer, we would patch the cracks, and the chimney would be fine until the next freeze. We had had the chimney checked the first winter. A sweep came to clean the flue, and I asked him to check for any chimney damage. There was none.

So my husband and I kept patching the stucco each summer, confident that cosmetic damage was our only problem.

The morning the appraiser was scheduled to show

up, my husband took a walk around the house to check our recent repairs and see that everything was in order. When he rounded the south corner of the house, he saw a table-sized chunk of stucco lying on the ground, surrounded by pieces of what looked like cement. In the night a hard freeze had caused the stucco to peel off the chimney face, exposing a totally disintegrated layer of brick underneath. The timing couldn't have been worse.

Now what we had always considered a minor repair in our preparation to move had become a major expense.

The appraiser simply wrote on his form that day, "Repair chimney stucco," but when we sought estimates from several repairmen, they told us the problem was much worse than that. No one would repair the stucco; the brick underneath wouldn't support it. A far worse hazard had been exposed just before our move—the chimney itself was unstable and could collapse.

So we began getting estimates for rebuilding the entire chimney. I calculated we would still break even on the sale of the house if the chimney rebuilding didn't go higher than $800. That seemed awfully high at the time, but my heart really sank when I heard the estimates.

The last contractor that came out gave us the lowest bid—$3000.

Do the Right Thing

My husband and I talked it over. Our guiding principle thus far had always been: Do it right, from the highest viewpoint possible.

If we did our best at each decision point, working economically and fairly within the spiritual laws, then things would work out. We trusted this totally and hadn't been disappointed thus far, but it seemed now the principle was no longer working.

For a few days, as we read the estimates and analyzed our financial situation, we toyed with the thought of asking the new owners to pay part of the bill. After all, we would be out of the house in a few weeks, and they would have years of enjoying the new chimney. Wouldn't it be fair and economical to present this cost as an added-in condition of the sale?

The more we tossed around this idea, the worse I felt.

My stomach had been an indicator throughout the process of selling our house—if I felt the least bit queasy about an option, there was something spiritually not right about it. Other people might get a headache, have a minor accident, or hear an inner voice. I got an upset stomach. And my stomach was really acting up now.

Following the spiritual principle of "Do what you have agreed to do," I realized that the cleanest action spiritually was to accept the caved-in chimney as our responsibility and take care of it.

We had the money, although it would wipe out much of our savings. So the next week we hired a contractor, and the work began. He agreed to our conditions: the new chimney had to be finished within seven days so we could close on the house.

Unexpected Protection

About that time, there was a streak of below-zero weather, but the contractor kept to his word, and the

150

work continued under a tent of plastic sheeting wrapped around the scaffolding. They had to tear into the chimney foundation and pull away all the layers of brick.

By Monday, they were finished, and the appraiser signed off on our repairs.

The incident passed, swept away by new decision points and events that cropped up each day with the new house we were buying. I didn't think much about the chimney. The amount of $3000 only popped into my mind whenever I reviewed our depleted savings account.

The day we signed the final papers for the purchase of our new house, we stopped by the post office to pick up some mail. There was an envelope from my literary agent.

Inside was a check for just under $3000 made out to me!

I was flabbergasted. A royalty payment for my third book usually arrived every four or five months, but I'd forgotten that one was due. Not only that, but the two previous payments had been very small: $79 and $400, respectively. Nothing like $3000.

Suddenly the image of the $3000 chimney came into my mind. I began laughing out loud right there in the post office, then I ran out to the car to show my husband the good news.

Our Highest State

This was proof positive that Divine Spirit, the ECK, was protecting us as long as we were willing to work cleanly and honorably with life. Because we had done what we agreed to do with no expectation of being bailed out, Spirit had brought us the means to rebalance our life and take care of the unexpected problem.

Key to this experience for me was (1) doing what I had agreed to do, and (2) having no expectations of being bailed out at the eleventh hour.

To be full participants with Divine Spirit as Co-workers, we must be fully aware of our place in the order of life. As this awareness grows, we actually have fewer desires concerning the outcome of situations. And when we let go of desire, divine protection is given.

I had to give up my desire to "get back the money we were losing" paying for the chimney. Working from the highest state, we no longer want more money, more love, more this, more that.

We begin to have total trust in God that the correct outcome will be provided as long as we stay aligned with the highest state of being.

☼ Exercise: Seeking the Highest

Take a minute and ask yourself about any experience in your life: What can this experience teach me about myself and life? What is the highest state I can hold within this experience?

My husband's and my highest state during our chimney story was: We want to do what is fair, economical, and spiritually clean.

Whatever your highest state, if you can hold it during challenging times, God will provide the best possible outcome.

Search for a Cello Player

ECKANKAR's seminar manager told me a fascinating story about a problem that arose at one of ECKANKAR's major seminars. The seminar was to begin on a Friday morning. Thursday, the lead cello player called long distance. She had thrown her back out and would be staying at home in bed instead of playing in the ensemble. It appeared impossible to find last-minute replacements for the difficult pieces to be played on Sunday. Here's how the story worked out, in my friend's words.

"Just before the seminar, I had asked what I could do to be the best vehicle for the ECK. The answer I got was deceptively simple: Just do all the things that you are asked to do. I mulled over this insight and decided I could commit to it.

"I would do everything that was asked of me during the next four days.

"Thursday afternoon I was standing in the central office where we coordinate all the functions of the seminar. A staff member came up to me and asked, 'Do you have a refrigerator in your room?'

"Most of the hotel rooms had no refrigerators. But my room happened to have one. I said, 'Well, actually, yes.'

"She then handed me a paper bag. 'Would you take my lunch for tomorrow over to your hotel and put it in the refrigerator?' she asked.

"I was nonplussed. There was so much to do, and the hotel was a good ten-minute walk. The errand would take a costly half hour. Not to mention that

I'd have to turn over my room key so she could fetch the bag early next morning. The whole thing felt uncomfortable, and I was about to refuse.

"But something made me hesitate for a moment. And in that moment, I remembered my promise. Do everything I was asked to do.

"So I took the bag and headed for the skyway to the hotel. I was grumbling to myself a little as I walked.

"Once at the hotel I ran into the composer of one of the ensemble pieces. Face aglow, he said, 'I'm so happy to have that incredibly skilled cello player coming. My whole piece really depends on the cello melody.'

"I didn't have the heart to tell him that the player had just canceled. I shifted back and forth on my feet and smiled weakly.

"He continued, 'Of course there's a woman here all the way from Brisbane, Australia, who's also incredible on cello. She plays in the symphony. Her name is Kaja.'

"At that moment the walkie-talkie crackled in my ear. It was a coworker with a message for the bookroom manager. 'We have a volunteer here who would like to work in the bookroom,' he announced. 'Her name is Kaja, and she's from Australia.'

"I couldn't believe the timing. I immediately got on the air and had my coworker detain Kaja for a few minutes, explaining our dilemma.

"She said she would be happy to help, but she had no cello with her.

"I put the lunch in the refrigerator, wondering at the divine timing involved in meeting the composer and hearing about Kaja—all over a lunch bag.

"The miracle continued from there. 'Well, we've

just found a cello player,' I announced to general cheers back at the central office. 'Now we just have to get on the phone and call every music store to find her a cello.'

"The news was not good. Minimum rental was $225 for a student-grade cello—basically a cardboard box with strings to a skilled player.

"We told Kaja of our problem, and she decided to call the local Minnesota orchestra. Amazingly enough, she connected with the lead cellist, who was interested in her situation. He agreed to meet her outside Orchestra Hall, convenient to the seminar location.

"Kaja went to an ECK Musicians Group meeting at a local hotel and sat down to enjoy the speakers. After a while she heard someone say, 'Just two more minutes,' and thinking the meeting was over, got up to leave. She was out the door by the time she figured out that the two-minute warning was for one of the speakers. But she went outside anyway.

"There she ran into a Japanese fellow. It was the cellist from the Minnesota orchestra.

"They walked back to the seminar hall together, and he asked her about ECKANKAR. By the time they arrived, he was fascinated with what she was telling him, and happy to loan Kaja a priceless German cello.

"For me the gift of this entire experience was in being able to perform the small, menial task of taking someone's lunch over to the hotel—and seeing the ECK use it and me for a much greater purpose."

Being a participant in miracles like this one means you are naturally in the right place at the right time. My friend was in the right place to meet the composer; in the story I told in chapter 5 about finding my dream house, I just happened to be passing it that day when the real estate agent was putting on the lock box. Five minutes earlier or later wouldn't have worked for either of us.

Working with Life's Rhythm

In a 1988 article in *Writer's Digest* magazine, author Natalie Goldberg talks about how paying slow and careful attention to life is essential to becoming a good writer. "In slowing down," she says, "you can experience the space in every situation and the opportunity inherent there." Slowing down and paying attention allows each person to see the natural rhythm in his or her life.

I've found that turning points in my life also have a certain rhythm.

When I move through life quickly and carelessly these turning points speed by in a blur—and life catches me unaware when the cumulative price of change hits. I've seen this in others as the much-discussed midlife crisis, where someone shucks stability to ride their motorcycle down a deserted highway.

Many turning points are happening within our lives all the time on different levels: the larger turning points of birth, adolescence, marriage, parenting, aging, and death; the smaller ones that move within the years, months, days, and minutes.

Goldberg is talking about focusing on the smaller turning points to be more fluid within the larger ones. This is a real key to training ourselves to be a Co-worker with God.

Steps to Change

But how do we start to see the smaller turning points within larger ones?

One way is by looking carefully at each step that leads up to a change. Authors like Joseph Campbell and Gloria Karpinski believe that any major change encompasses smaller steps. Campbell's hero's journey includes a call to adventure and vision quest, tests and trials, the return of the hero, and the integration of lessons learned into daily life.

Karpinski says that once our basic belief system, the status quo in our lives, is challenged, the dance of transformation begins.

The process often includes specific steps: overcoming the wall of inner resistance to find a new understanding; commitment to the new direction and a time of testing our faith by some ordeal; and accepting the transformation.

Remember my turning point in chapter 1, where I was learning to slow down with my work? I went through very specific steps in realizing what was happening and navigating the turning point. First came my old belief that I was valuable to the job only as a producer of materials, and an efficient one at that. Then I encountered the problem with my arm— I could no longer work fast and furiously. I knew a turning point was coming, but I resisted it mightily because I couldn't see how I could be valued if I didn't produce.

Next came a new understanding: my coeditor telling me it really was OK to slow down; in fact it was preferable because she could no longer keep up with me.

What a revelation! Maybe I could be a valued worker without being a production machine. This brought a sense of commitment. I was now eager to see how to fully wear this new role at work. My ears were open for a clue, which was so happily provided by my friend at lunch that week.

The next stage, an ordeal which tested my faith, began with my afternoon appointment with the acupuncturist.

I had made a 2:30 p.m. appointment but had forgotten the 3:00 holiday party at work. When I arrived for the party fifteen minutes late, the front doors were locked. No one had remembered to let me know the party was being held in a downstairs room, out of sight of the doors. The building manager had decided to lock up early rather than sit upstairs and miss the fun.

I'm still working on the final stage of this turning point, acceptance of a new way of being. I believe this will last a lifetime, as I translate my new knowledge into working every day.

☀ Exercise: Your Own Steps to Change

Using the steps outlined above or ones based on your own past experience, chart your own journey through a change.

Analyze a recent turning point, whether large or small, inner or outer, using these steps. Can you find the steps within the turning point?

This is especially helpful when you meet a difficult turning point or one that you don't understand. Look to the past, and try this exercise on any change that still puzzles you.

Golden Flowers

Midway through my experience with learning to slow down at work, an unexpected gift appeared on my desk one morning. It was a potted plant of freesias. I had admired them in my coworker's office the day before. They were fragrant, pale-lilac flowers with golden centers.

Surely a sign, I thought at the time, *but of what?*

The freesias lasted ten days. Each morning I enjoyed their heavenly fragrance and color, and as I clipped the spent blossoms I realized a major change had come to me, marked by the life of the plant. I had turned a corner.

I was feeling a lot better about myself at work. The days no longer went by in a blur of machinelike production, and I still had a stack of edited books to show I'd been busy.

I realized with a smile that the freesias had been my own private symbol for the past week or so, reminding me to "stop and smell the flowers."

Who says Divine Spirit doesn't have a sense of humor?

Stay Tuned

Divine Spirit makes Itself known to us in ways we can handle at any one time—sometimes in humorous ways like my freesias, other times in more serious ways. Each time we are ready for a new and finer level of awareness about our lives and how to welcome the next turning points, the details of

159

that level emerge. Like climbing a ladder, each step offers a viewpoint, as well as new spiritual laws to learn.

Moving up spiritually is a process of learning how to see and be at each new level. And each time we move up, we drop old habits that are no longer needed.

This is the essence of a turning point. And it is not an easy process.

The key is staying tuned to Divine Spirit's guidance, and to the rhythm of life. This brings true spiritual freedom—a level beyond coping, beyond getting through each day.

It brings us the ability to relax as God carries us safely home.

Whenever I doubt the presence of Divine Spirit in turning points, I remember that night at nineteen, when I was crossing the lake in the Ozarks at sunset. I remember my feelings of uncertainty—how the ferry carrying my car looked too small, too unsteady, without any security in railings on the sides. The water looked choppy at first, but I remember how it smoothed out as we passed the bend of islands in the middle of the lake.

It may look safer to stay onshore or find a longer, harder way around each turning point that comes. But the view from the middle of the lake is much better than the one from shore. And the more times I travel across, the more I trust that I will reach the other side.

The horizon always looks different from there, but there is also an exciting new road to travel.

Glossary

Words set in SMALL CAPS are defined elsewhere in this glossary.

ARAHATA. An experienced and qualified teacher for ECKANKAR classes.

CHELA. A spiritual student.

ECK. The Life Force, the Holy Spirit, or Audible Life Current which sustains all life.

ECKANKAR. Religion of the Light and Sound of God. Also known as the Ancient Science of SOUL TRAVEL. A truly spiritual religion for the individual in modern times, known as the secret path to God via dreams and SOUL TRAVEL. The teachings provide a framework for anyone to explore their own spiritual experiences. Established by Paul Twitchell, the modern-day founder, in 1965.

ECK MASTERS. Spiritual Masters who can assist and protect people in their spiritual studies and travels. The ECK Masters are from a long line of God-Realized SOULS who know the responsibility that goes with spiritual freedom.

HU. The most ancient, secret name for God. The singing of the word HU, pronounced like the word *hue,* is considered a love song to God. It is sung in the ECK Worship Service.

INITIATION. Earned by the ECK member through spiritual unfoldment and service to God. The initiation is a private ceremony in which the individual is linked to the Sound and Light of God.

LIVING ECK MASTER. The title of the spiritual leader of ECKANKAR. His duty is to lead SOULS back to God. The Living ECK Master can assist spiritual students physically

161

as the Outer Master, in the dream state as the Dream Master, and in the spiritual worlds as the Inner Master. Sri Harold Klemp became the MAHANTA, the Living ECK Master in 1981.

MAHANTA. A title to describe the highest state of God Consciousness on earth, often embodied in the LIVING ECK MASTER. He is the Living Word.

PLANES. The levels of heaven, such as the Astral, Causal, Mental, Etheric, and Soul planes.

SATSANG. A class in which students of ECK study a monthly lesson from ECKANKAR.

THE SHARIYAT-KI-SUGMAD. The sacred scriptures of ECKANKAR. The scriptures are comprised of twelve volumes in the spiritual worlds. The first two were transcribed from the inner PLANES by Paul Twitchell, modern-day founder of ECKANKAR.

SOUL. The True Self. The inner, most sacred part of each person. Soul exists before birth and lives on after the death of the physical body. As a spark of God, Soul can see, know, and perceive all things. It is the creative center of Its own world.

SOUL TRAVEL. The expansion of consciousness. The ability of SOUL to transcend the physical body and travel into the spiritual worlds of God. Soul Travel is taught only by the LIVING ECK MASTER. It helps people unfold spiritually and can provide proof of the existence of God and life after death.

SOUND AND LIGHT OF ECK. The Holy Spirit. The two aspects through which God appears in the lower worlds. People can experience them by looking and listening within themselves and through SOUL TRAVEL.

SPIRITUAL EXERCISES OF ECK. The daily practice of certain techniques to get us in touch with the Light and Sound of God.

SUGMAD. A sacred name for God. SUGMAD is neither masculine nor feminine; IT is the source of all life.

WAH Z. The spiritual name of Sri Harold Klemp. It means the Secret Doctrine. It is his name in the spiritual worlds.

162

Bibliography

Ann Archer, "The Power of 'HU,' " 1986 *ECK Mata Journal* (Volume 10): 5, 28.

Joseph V. Bailey, *The Serenity Principle: Finding Inner Peace in Recovery* (San Francisco: Harper & Row, Publishers, Inc., 1990).

Frances Blackwell, "Love Never Dies," 1994 *ECKANKAR Journal* (Volume 18): 29–31.

Deepak Chopra, M.D., and Judith Sills, Ph.D., "How to Be Your Best in '94." McCall's, January 1994, 105–6.

Phil Cousineau, editor, *The Hero's Journey: The World of Joseph Campbell* (San Francisco: Harper & Row, Publishers, Inc., 1990).

Jeff Davidson, *Breathing Space: Living and Working at a Comfortable Pace in a Sped-Up Society* (New York: MasterMedia Limited, 1991).

Natalie Goldberg, "Slowing Down." *Writer's Digest,* August 1988, 39–40.

Barbara Hey, "Changing Times." *SELF,* August 1989, 150–55.

Richard Hugo, *The Triggering Town* (New York: W.W. Norton & Company, Inc., 1979).

Gloria Karpinski, *Where Two Worlds Touch* (New York: Ballantine Books, 1990).

Ralph Keyes, *Chancing It* (New York: Little, Brown & Co., 1985).

Harold Klemp, "Turning Points," The *Mystic World,* Spring 1992.

_____, *Ask the Master,* Book Two (Minneapolis: ECKANKAR, 1994).

_____, *The Spiritual Exercises of ECK* (Minneapolis: ECKANKAR, 1993).

Robert Redford, "Family Values." *Vogue,* November 1992, 149–52.

Gabriele Lusser Rico, *Writing the Natural Way* (Los Angeles: J. P. Tarcher, Inc., 1983).

_____, *Pain and Possibility* (Los Angeles: Jeremy P. Tarcher, Inc., 1991).

Catherine Watson, "In Borneo, a Blessing Disguised as a Curse." *Minneapolis Star Tribune,* 26 September 1993, 1G, 3G.

How to Take the Next Step on Your Spiritual Journey

Find your own answers to questions about your past, present, and future through the ancient wisdom of ECKANKAR. Take the next bold step on your spiritual journey.

ECKANKAR can show you why special attention from God is neither random nor only for a few saints. It is for anyone who opens his heart to Divine Spirit, the Light and Sound of God.

Are you looking for the secrets of life and the afterlife? Sri Harold Klemp, today's spiritual leader of ECKANKAR, and Paul Twitchell, its modern-day founder, have written a series of monthly discourses that give unique Spiritual Exercises of ECK. They can lead you in a direct way to God. Those who join ECKANKAR, Religion of the Light and Sound of God, can receive these monthly discourses.

As a Member of ECKANKAR You'll Discover

1. The most direct route home to God through the ECK teachings of the Light and Sound. Plus the opportunity to gain wisdom, charity, and spiritual freedom in this lifetime through the ECK initiations.

2. The spiritual meaning of dreams, Soul Travel techniques, and ways to establish a personal relationship with Divine Spirit through study of monthly discourses. These discourses are for the entire family. You may study them alone at home or in a class with others.

3. Secrets of self-mastery in a Wisdom Note and articles by the Living ECK Master in the *Mystic World,* a quarterly newsletter. In it are also letters and articles from ECK members around the world.

4. Upcoming ECK seminars and other activities worldwide, new study materials from ECKANKAR, and more, in special mailings. Join the excitement. Have the fulfilling experience of attending major ECK seminars!

5. The joy of the ECK Satsang (discourse study) experience in classes and book discussions. Share spiritual experiences and find answers to your questions about the ECK teachings.

How to Find Out More

To request membership in ECKANKAR using your credit card (or for a free booklet on membership) call (612) 544-0066, weekdays, between 8:00 a.m. and 5:00 p.m., central time. Or write to: ECKANKAR, Att: Information, P.O. Box 27300, Minneapolis, MN 55427 U.S.A.

Introductory Books on ECKANKAR

What Is Spiritual Freedom?
Mahanta Transcripts, Book 11
Harold Klemp

You make your heaven here and now. The more you understand this, the greater your spiritual freedom. Through stories and twenty-three techniques, Harold Klemp shows how to get to the spiritual root of your problems and take your next step on the road to spiritual freedom.

ECKANKAR—Ancient Wisdom for Today
Are you one of the millions who have heard God speak to you through a profound spiritual experience? This introductory book will show you how dreams, Soul Travel, and experiences with past lives are ways God speaks to you. An entertaining, easy-to-read approach to ECKANKAR. Reading this little book can give you new perspectives on your spiritual life.

The Spiritual Exercises of ECK
The Book of ECK Parables, Volume 4
Harold Klemp

This book is a staircase with 131 steps. It's a special staircase, because you don't have to climb all the steps to get to the top. Each step is a spiritual exercise, a way to help you explore your inner worlds. And what awaits you at the top? The doorway to spiritual freedom, self-mastery, wisdom, and love.

HU: A Love Song to God
(Audiocassette)

Learn how to sing an ancient name for God, HU (pronounced like the word *hue*). A wonderful introduction to ECKANKAR, this two-tape set is designed to help listeners of any religious or philosophical background benefit from the gifts of the Holy Spirit. It includes an explanation of the HU, stories about how Divine Spirit works in daily life, and exercises to uplift you spiritually.

For fastest service, phone **(612) 544-0066** weekdays between 8 a.m. and 5 p.m., central time, to request books using your credit card, or look under **ECKANKAR** in your phone book for an ECKANKAR Center near you. Or write: **ECKANKAR, Att: Information, P.O. Box 27300, Minneapolis, MN 55427 U.S.A.**

There May Be an
ECKANKAR Study Group near You

ECKANKAR offers a variety of local and international activities for the spiritual seeker. With hundreds of study groups worldwide, ECKANKAR is near you! Many areas have ECKANKAR Centers where you can browse through the books in a quiet, unpressured environment, talk with others who share an interest in this ancient teaching, and attend beginning discussion classes on how to gain the attributes of Soul: wisdom, power, love, and freedom.

Around the world, ECKANKAR study groups offer special one-day or weekend seminars on the basic teachings of ECKANKAR. Check your phone book under **ECKANKAR**, ☎ or call **(612) 544-0066** for membership information and the location of the ECKANKAR Center or study group nearest you. Or write **ECKANKAR, Att: Information, P.O. Box 27300, Minneapolis, MN 55427 U.S.A.**

☐ Please send me information on the nearest ECKANKAR Center or study group in my area.

☐ Please send me more information about membership in ECKANKAR, which includes a twelve-month spiritual study.

Please type or print clearly   817

Name _____

Street _____ Apt. # _____

City _____ State/Prov. _____

ZIP/Postal Code _____ Country _____